# FIX-IT and FORGET-IT®
## *Favorite*
# SLOW COOKER RECIPES FOR DAD

## 150 Recipes Dad Will Love to Make, Eat, and Share!

# HOPE COMERFORD

Photos by Bonnie Matthews

## Good Books
New York, New York

Good Books books may be purchased in bulk at special discounts for sales promotion, corporate gifts, fund-raising, or educational purposes. Special editions can also be created to specifications. For details, contact the Special Sales Department, Good Books, 307 West 36th Street, 11th Floor, New York, NY 10018 or info@skyhorsepublishing.com.

Good Books is an imprint of Skyhorse Publishing, Inc.®, a Delaware corporation.

Visit our website at www.goodbooks.com.

10 9 8 7 6 5 4 3 2

Library of Congress Cataloging-in-Publication Data is available on file.

Cover design by Jenny Zemanek

Print ISBN: 978-1-68099-287-8
Ebook ISBN: 978-1-68099-295-3

Printed in China

To all the amazing men in my life, who have loved me and supported me, cooked for me or have let me cook for them, guided me, inspired me, and cheered me on—thank you!

# Table of Contents

# Welcome to Fix-It and Forget-It Favorite Slow Cooker Recipes for Dad

We once again reached out to Team Fix-It and Forget-It, this time to ask them for their favorite and most popular recipes for Dad. The end result? 150 tasty and Dad-approved recipes. Let's be honest. Dads like simple. What could be simpler than putting ingredients into your slow cooker, turning it on, then coming back to something delicious? These recipes will not only satisfy Dad's hunger, but they'll also help him feel confident in the kitchen. So, Dads, whether you're making breakfast for the family, snacks for your buddies, dinner for your whole crew, or dessert to sweeten up your sweet(s), we've got you covered! All right, Dads . . . go get your slow cookin' on! You've got this!

## Choosing a Slow Cooker

### Not all slow cookers are created equal . . . or work equally as well for everyone!

Those of us who use slow cookers frequently know we have our own preferences when it comes to which slow cooker we choose to use. For instance, I love my programmable slow cooker, but there are many programmable slow cookers I've tried that I've strongly disliked. Why? Because some go by increments of 15 or 30 minutes and some go by 4, 6, 8, or 10 hours. I dislike those restrictions, but I have family and friends who don't mind them at all! I am also pretty brand loyal when it comes to my manual slow cookers because I've had great success with those and have had unsuccessful moments with slow cookers of other brands. So, which slow cooker(s) is/are best for your household?

It really depends on how many people you're feeding and if you're gone for long periods of time. Here are my recommendations:

| For 2–3 person household | 3–5 quart slow cooker |
| For 4–5 person household | 5–6 quart slow cooker |
| For a 6+ person household | 6½–7 quart slow cooker |

## Large slow cooker advantages/disadvantages:

Advantages:
- You can fit a loaf pan or a baking dish into a 6- or 7-quart, depending on the shape of your cooker. That allows you to make bread or cakes, or even smaller quantities of main dishes. (Take your favorite baking dish and loaf pan along when you shop for a cooker to make sure they'll fit inside.)
- You can feed large groups of people, or make larger quantities of food, allowing for leftovers, or meals, to freeze.

Disadvantages:
- They take up more storage room.
- They don't fit as neatly into a dishwasher.
- If your crock isn't ⅔–¾ full, you may burn your food.

## Small slow cooker advantages/disadvantages:

Advantages:
- They're great for lots of appetizers, for serving hot drinks, for baking cakes straight in the crock, and for dorm rooms or apartments.
- Great option for making recipes of smaller quantities.

Disadvantages:
- Food in smaller quantities tends to cook more quickly than larger amounts. So keep an eye on it.
- Chances are, you won't have many leftovers. So, if you like to have leftovers, a smaller slow cooker may not be a good option for you.

## My recommendation:

Have at least two slow cookers; one around 3 to 4 quarts and one 6 quarts or larger. A third would be a huge bonus (and a great advantage to your cooking repertoire!). The advantage of having at least a couple is you can make a larger variety of recipes. Also, you can make at least two or three dishes at once for a whole meal.

# Manual vs. Programmable

If you are gone for only six to eight hours a day, a manual slow cooker might be just fine for you. If you are gone for more than eight hours during the day, I would highly recommend purchasing a programmable slow cooker that will switch to warm when the cook time you set is up. It will allow you to cook a wider variety of recipes.

The two I use most frequently are my 4-quart manual slow cooker and my 6½-quart programmable slow cooker. I like that I can make smaller portions in my 4-quart slow cooker on days I don't need or want leftovers, but I also love how my 6½-quart slow cooker can accommodate whole chickens, turkey breasts, hams, or big batches of soups. I use them both often.

# Get to Know Your Slow Cooker . . .

Plan a little time to get acquainted with your slow cooker. Each slow cooker has its own personality—just like your oven (and your car). Plus, many new slow cookers cook hotter and faster than earlier models. I think that with all of the concern for food safety, the slow cooker manufacturers have amped up their settings so that "High," "Low," and "Warm" are all higher temperatures than in the older models. That means they cook hotter—and therefore, faster—than the first slow cookers. The beauty of these little machines is that they're supposed to cook low and slow. We count on that when we flip the switch in the morning before we leave the house for ten hours or so. So, because none of us knows what kind of temperament our slow cooker has until we try it out, nor how hot it cooks—don't assume anything. Save yourself a disappointment and make the first recipe in your new slow cooker on a day when you're at home. Cook it for the shortest amount of time the recipe calls for. Then, check the food to see if it's done. Or if you start smelling food that seems to be finished, turn off the cooker and rescue your food.

Also, all slow cookers seem to have a "hot spot," which is of great importance to know, especially when baking with your slow cooker. This spot may tend to burn food in that area if you're not careful. If you're baking directly in your slow cooker, I recommend covering the "hot spot" with some foil.

# Take Notes . . .

Don't be afraid to make notes in your cookbook. It's yours! Chances are, it will eventually get passed down to someone in your family and they will love and appreciate all of your musings. Take note of which slow cooker you used and exactly how long it took to cook the recipe. The next time you make it, you won't need to try to remember. Apply what you learned to the next recipes you make in your cooker. If another recipe says it needs to cook 7–9 hours, and you've discovered your slow cooker cooks on the faster side, cook that recipe for 6–6½ hours and then check it. You can always cook a recipe longer—but you can't reverse things if it's overdone.

# Get Creative . . .

If you know your morning is going to be hectic, prepare everything the night before, take it out of the fridge when you first get up in the morning so the crock warms up to room temperature, then plug it in and turn it on as you're leaving the house.

If you want to make something that has a short cook time and you're going to be gone longer than that, cook it the night before and refrigerate it for the next day. Warm it up when you get home. Or, cook those recipes on the weekend when you know you'll be home and eat them later in the week.

# Slow Cooking Tips and Tricks and Other Things You May Not Know

- Slow cookers tend to work best when they're ⅔ to ¾ of the way full. You may need to increase the cooking time if you've exceeded that amount, or reduce it if you've put in less than that. If you're going to exceed that limit, it would be best to reduce the recipe, or split it between two slow cookers. (Remember how I suggested owning at least two or three slow cookers?)

- Keep your veggies on the bottom. That puts them in more direct contact with the heat. The fuller your slow cooker, the longer it will take its contents to cook. Also, the more densely packed the cooker's contents are, the longer they will take to cook. And finally, the larger the chunks of meat or vegetables, the more time they will need to cook.

- Keep the lid on! Every time you take a peek, you lose 20 minutes of cooking time. Please take this into consideration each time you lift the lid! I know, some of you can't help yourself and are going to lift anyway. Just don't forget to tack on 20 minutes to your cook time for each time you peeked!

- Sometimes it's beneficial to remove the lid. If you'd like your dish to thicken a bit, take the lid off during the last half hour to hour of cooking time.

- If you have a big slow cooker (7- to 8-quart), you can cook a small batch in it by putting the recipe ingredients into an oven-safe baking dish or baking pan and then placing that into the cooker's crock. First, put a trivet or some metal jar rings on the bottom of the crock, and then set your dish or pan on top of them. Or a loaf pan may "hook on to" the top ridges of the crock belonging to a large oval cooker and hang there straight and securely, "baking" a cake or quick bread. Cover the cooker and flip it on.

- The outside of your slow cooker will be hot! Please remember to keep it out of reach of children and keep that in mind for yourself as well!
- Get yourself a quick-read meat thermometer and use it! This helps remove the question of whether or not your meat is fully cooked, and helps prevent you from overcooking your meat as well.

  **Internal cooking temperatures:**
  - Beef—125–130°F (rare); 140–145°F (medium); 160°F (well-done)
  - Pork—140–145°F (rare); 145–150°F (medium); 160°F (well-done)
  - Turkey and chicken—165°F
- Frozen Meat: The basic rule of thumb is, don't put frozen meat into the slow cooker. The meat does not reach the proper internal temperature in time. This especially applies to thick cuts of meat! Proceed with caution!
- Add fresh herbs 10 minutes before the end of the cooking time to maximize their flavor.
- If your recipe calls for cooked pasta, add it 10 minutes before the end of the cooking time if the cooker is on High; 30 minutes before the end of the cooking time if it's on Low. Then the pasta won't get mushy.
- If your recipe calls for sour cream or cream, stir it in 5 minutes before the end of the cooking time. You want it to heat but not boil or simmer.

  **Approximate slow cooker temperatures (remember, each slow cooker is different):**
  - High—212°F–300°F
  - Low—170°F–200°F
  - Simmer—185°F
  - Warm—165°F

  **Cooked and dried bean measurements:**
  - 16-oz. can, drained = about 1¾ cups beans
  - 19-oz. can, drained = about 2 cups beans
  - 1 lb. dried beans (about 2½ cups) = 5 cups cooked beans

Breakfasts

# Smokey Sausage and Sweet Pepper Hash

Hope Comerford, Clinton Township, MI

*Makes 6–8 servings*
*Prep. Time: 10 minutes* ⚜ *Cooking Time: 6 hours* ⚜ *Ideal slow-cooker size: 4-qt.*

12-oz. pkg. smoked sausages, cut lengthwise, then into ½-inch pieces

16 oz. frozen diced potatoes

1½ cups sweet onion, sliced

1 yellow pepper, sliced

1 green pepper, sliced

1 red pepper, sliced

¼ cup melted butter

1 tsp. salt

½ tsp. pepper

½ tsp. dried thyme

½ tsp. dried parsley

1 cup shredded Swiss cheese

**1.** Spray crock with nonstick spray.

**2.** Place sausage, frozen potatoes, onions, and sliced peppers into crock.

**3.** Mix melted butter with salt, pepper, thyme and parsley. Pour over contents of crock and stir.

**4.** Cover and cook on Low for 6 hours. Sprinkle with the Swiss cheese, then cover and cook for an additional 20 minutes, or until the cheese is melted.

# Top-of-the-Morning Sausage and Dumplings

*MarJanita Geigley, Lancaster, PA*

**Makes 6 servings**

*Prep. Time: 30 minutes* ♣ *Cooking Time: 4 hours* ♣ *Ideal slow-cooker size: 5-qt.*

½ large onion, chopped

1½ tsp. butter

4 cups chopped cooked sausage

10¾-oz. can cream of mushroom soup

1 cup sour cream

½ cup milk

½ cup chopped green peppers

½ cup diced tomatoes

1 cup shredded cheese

6 refrigerator canned biscuits, cut into halves

**1.** Combine all ingredients except biscuits into slow cooker.

**2.** Cook on Low for 2 hours.

**3.** Top with biscuit halves so entire top is covered.

**4.** Cook for 2 hours longer.

# Cheesy Hash Brown Breakfast Bake

*Hope Comerford, Clinton Township, MI*

*Makes 6–8 servings*
*Prep. Time: 15 minutes ⚬ Cooking Time: 7–8 hours ⚬ Ideal slow-cooker size: 5-qt.*

10¾-oz. can cream of chicken soup

1 cup sour cream

6 eggs

1 tsp. garlic powder

¼ tsp. salt

¼ tsp. pepper

1 small onion, minced

8 oz. precooked ham steak, cut into tiny cubes

2 lb. frozen hash browns

2 cups shredded cheddar cheese

syrup, *optional*

**1.** Spray your crock with nonstick spray.

**2.** Mix together the soup, sour cream, eggs, garlic powder, salt and pepper.

**3.** Add the onion, ham, hash browns, and cheese and stir until well-mixed.

**4.** Pour this mixture into your crock.

**5.** Cover and cook on Low for 7–8 hours.

**6.** If desired, serve with syrup drizzled over the top.

# Cheesy Ranch Tater Tot Bake

*Hope Comerford, Clinton Township, MI*

*Makes 6–8 servings*
Prep. Time: 10 minutes  &  Cooking Time: 7–9 hours  &  Ideal slow-cooker size: 6-qt.

1 lb. ground turkey, browned

½ cup onion, chopped

2 cups shredded cheddar cheese

32-oz. bag frozen Tater Tots

10¾-oz. can condensed cheddar cheese soup

10¾-oz. can condensed cream of chicken soup

1 tsp. onion powder

1 cup milk

1-oz. packet dry ranch dressing mix

**1.** Spray your crock with nonstick spray.

**2.** Line the bottom of your crock with the ground turkey.

**3.** Sprinkle the onions on top of the turkey.

**4.** Spread the cheese over the onions.

**5.** Spread the Tater Tots on top of the onions.

**6.** Mix together the cheddar cheese soup, the cream of chicken soup, onion powder, milk, and ranch dressing seasoning mix. Pour this over the top of the Tater Tots in the crock and spread evenly.

**7.** Cover and cook on Low for 7–9 hours.

**TIP**
This makes an excellent breakfast, lunch, or dinner!

# Mexican Breakfast Casserole

Hope Comerford, Clinton Township, MI

*Makes 4 servings*
Prep. Time: 20 minutes  ⚵  Cooking Time: 7–8 hours  ⚵  Ideal slow-cooker size: 3-qt.

8 eggs

1 ½ cups milk

1 tsp. salt

1 tsp. pepper

¾ cup picante sauce (such as Pace Mild®)—this equals about half a jar

1 small onion, chopped

½ jalapeño pepper, seeds removed, minced

1 cup frozen corn

2 cups shredded Mexican blend cheese, *divided*

9 (or more) white corn tortillas (5¾-inch recommended)

7 oz. (or so) chorizo, removed from the casing, *divided*

1. Mix together the eggs, milk, salt, pepper, picante sauce, onions, jalapeño, corn, and 1 cup shredded Mexican blend cheese.

2. Spray your crock with nonstick spray.

3. Line the bottom of the crock with approximately 3 white corn tortillas.

4. Pour half of the egg mixture over this and then crumble half of the chorizo on top. Repeat this process with another layer of tortillas, egg mixture, and the remaining chorizo.

5. Top with a final layer of tortillas and the remaining cheese on top.

6. Cover and cook on Low for 7–8 hours.

TIP
If you can't find chorizo, try mild or spicy Italian ground sausage instead.

# Breakfast Polenta with Bacon

*Margaret W. High, Lancaster, PA*

*Makes 8–10 servings*
*Prep. Time: 20 minutes  ❧  Cooking Time: 2½ hours  ❧  Ideal slow-cooker size: 5–6 qt.*

4 eggs, room temperature

2 cups whole milk, room temperature

2 cups stone-ground (coarse) cornmeal

⅔ cup shredded Parmesan cheese, *divided*

½ cup cooked, diced bacon

2 Tbsp. finely diced onion

2 cups chopped fresh spinach

1 tsp. salt

pepper, to taste

4 cups boiling water

**1.** In a large mixing bowl, beat eggs. Whisk in milk, cornmeal, and ⅓ cup Parmesan.

**2.** Whisk in boiling water.

**3.** Gently stir in bacon, onion, spinach, salt, and pepper.

**4.** Pour mixture into well-greased slow cooker.

**5.** Cover and cook on High for 2 hours, stirring once to be sure cornmeal is evenly distributed as it cooks.

**6.** When polenta is thick, sprinkle with remaining ⅓ cup Parmesan. Remove lid and allow to cook on High for an additional 30 minutes as cheese melts and any extra liquid evaporates. Polenta will be softer when hot, but will firm up as it cools. Serve hot, warm, or chilled.

**TIP**
If you're in a pinch, you can use real bacon-bits in place of the bacon. Fresh is always best though!

# Egg and Cheese Bake

*Evie Hershey, Atglen, PA*

**Makes 6 servings**
Prep. Time: 15 minutes   ❧   Cooking Time: 4–6 hours   ❧   Ideal slow-cooker size: 4-qt.

3 cups toasted bread cubes

1½ cups shredded cheese

½ cup fried, crumbled bacon, or ham chunks, *optional*

6 eggs, beaten

3 cups milk

¾ tsp. salt

¼ tsp. pepper

**1.** Combine bread cubes, cheese, and meat in greased slow cooker.

**2.** Mix together eggs, milk, salt, and pepper. Pour over bread.

**3.** Cook on Low 4–6 hours.

# Easy Egg and Sausage Puff

*Sara Kinsinger, Stuarts Draft, VA*

**Makes 6 servings**
*Prep. Time: 10–15 minutes  ❧  Cooking Time: 2–2½ hours  ❧  Ideal slow-cooker size: 2- to 4-qt.*

1 lb. loose sausage

6 eggs

1 cup all-purpose baking mix

1 cup shredded cheddar cheese

2 cups milk

¼ tsp. dry mustard, *optional*

**1.** Brown sausage in nonstick skillet. Break up chunks of meat as it cooks. Drain.

**2.** Meanwhile, spray interior of slow cooker with nonstick cooking spray.

**3.** Mix all ingredients in slow cooker.

**4.** Cover and cook on High 1 hour. Turn to Low and cook 1–1½ hours, or until the dish is fully cooked in the center.

# Cinnamon French Toast Casserole

*Hope Comerford, Clinton Township, MI*

*Makes 6–8 servings*

*Prep. Time: 12 hours 10 minutes* ⚜ *Cooking Time: 6–8 hours* ⚜ *Ideal slow-cooker size: 6-qt.*

2 16-oz. loaves cinnamon swirl bread, sliced into ½-inch pieces and left out overnight to go stale

1 dozen eggs

4 cups milk

¼ cup brown sugar

2 tsp. cinnamon

2 tsp. vanilla extract

¼ tsp. salt

Optional:

powdered sugar

whipped cream

syrup

**1.** Spray the slow cooker with nonstick spray.

**2.** Place all the bread in the slow cooker.

**3.** Mix together the eggs, milk, brown sugar, cinnamon, vanilla, and salt.

**4.** Pour the egg mixture over the bread.

**5.** Cover and cook on Low for 6–8 hours.

**6.** The last ½ hour or so, remove the lid.

**7.** Dust with powdered sugar, a dollop of whipped cream, and/or drizzle with syrup when serving, if desired.

## TIP

Don't skip letting the bread dry out overnight, or you'll have a very soggy casserole. If you're in a pinch, put it into a 350°F oven until it's slightly browned, then let it cool for 15–20 minutes.

# Overnight Oatmeal

*Lisa Clark, Chesterfield, MI*

**Makes 6 servings**
Prep. Time: 10 minutes   ⚹   Cooking Time: 8–9 hours   ⚹   Ideal slow-cooker size: 4½-qt.

2 whole sliced apples
¼ cup brown sugar
1 tsp. cinnamon
pinch salt
2 cups oatmeal
2 cups milk
2 cups water

1. Place sliced apples in bottom of crock.

2. Sprinkle apples with brown sugar, cinnamon, and salt.

3. On top of apples and spice, add oatmeal, milk, and water.

4. Do *not* stir.

5. Cover and cook overnight, 8–9 hours on Low.

# Oatmeal Morning

*Barbara Forrester Landis, Lititz, PA*

**Makes 6 servings**

*Prep. Time: 5 minutes* ⚙ *Cooking Time: 2½–6 hours* ⚙ *Ideal slow-cooker size: 3-qt.*

1 cup uncooked rolled oats

1 cup dried cranberries

2½ Tbsp. broken walnuts

½ tsp. salt

1 Tbsp. cinnamon

4 cups liquid—fat-free milk, water, or combination of the two

**1.** Combine all dry ingredients in slow cooker. Stir well.

**2.** Pour in liquid ingredient(s). Mix together well.

**3.** Cover. Cook on High 2½ hours, or on Low 5–6 hours.

**TIP**
If walnuts aren't your favorite, replace with a different kind of nut, or leave them out.

# Baked Oatmeal

*Juanita Weaver, Johnsonville, IL*

**Makes 4–6 servings**
*Prep. Time: 3 minutes    Cooking Time: 1 hour    Ideal slow-cooker size: 3-qt.*

1 stick butter
2 cups oatmeal
1 cup brown sugar
1 egg
1 tsp. baking powder
½ tsp. salt
1 tsp. vanilla extract
½ cup milk

1. Turn slow cooker on High.

2. Place butter in crock.

3. Measure all other ingredients in a bowl and stir with a fork till well mixed.

4. Pour mixture into slow cooker and stir lightly to mix some of the butter into the batter.

5. Cover and cook on High for 1 hour.

Serving suggestion:
This is wonderful served with blueberries and milk.

# Almond Date Oatmeal

*Audrey L. Kneer, Williamsfield, IL*

**Makes 8 servings**
*Prep. Time: 5 minutes* ⚶ *Cooking Time: 4–8 hours, or overnight* ⚶ *Ideal slow-cooker size: 3-qt.*

2 cups dry rolled oats
½ cup dry Grape-Nuts® cereal
½ cup chopped almonds
¼ cup chopped dates
4½ cups water

1. Combine all ingredients in slow cooker.

2. Cover and cook on Low 4–8 hours, or overnight.

Serving suggestion:
Serve with fat-free milk.

# Apple Cider Cinnamon Steel-Cut Oatmeal

*Jenny R. Unternahrer, Wayland, IA*

*Makes 3–4 servings*

*Prep. Time: 10 minutes ❧ Cooking Time: 5–6 hours ❧ Ideal slow-cooker size: 2-qt.*

3 medium Granny Smith apples, peeled and chopped

3½ cups apple cider

1 cup steel cut oats

¾ tsp. cinnamon

⅛ tsp. salt

3 Tbsp. sugar

**1.** Place a heat-safe baking dish inside your slow cooker. The heat transfers to the dish but doesn't seem to be as hot as the crock itself.

**2.** Place all of your ingredients into the dish and stir. Place lid on slow cooker and cook on Low for 5–6 hours.

**3.** The apples will still be on top but with a gentle stir it will combine nicely.

Serving suggestion:

Drizzle on a little pure maple syrup for some sweetness, top with chopped pecans or walnuts if you like, and enjoy!

# Cheese Grits

*Janie Steele, Moore, OK*

*Makes 6 servings*
*Prep. Time: 20 minutes  &  Cooking Time: 2–3 hours  &  Ideal slow-cooker size: 3–4-qt.*

4 cups water

1 tsp. salt

1 cup regular (not instant) grits, uncooked

3 eggs

4 Tbsp. (½ stick) butter, cut in chunks

1¾ cups grated sharp cheese

¼ tsp. pepper, *optional*

**1.** In saucepan, bring water and salt to boil. Slowly add grits, stirring.

**2.** Cook until grits are thick and creamy, 5–10 minutes.

**3.** Beat eggs in small bowl. Add spoonful of hot grits to eggs, stirring. This tempers the eggs.

**4.** Slowly stir egg mixture into rest of hot grits.

**5.** Add butter, cheese, and pepper (if using). Stir.

**6.** Pour grits into lightly greased slow cooker. Cook on High 2–3 hours until set in middle and lightly browned around edges.

## TIPS
Serve with eggs for breakfast or brunch, or serve with cooked greens and black-eyed peas for supper. Excellent topped with a juicy barbecue beef.

# Granola

*Hope Comerford, Clinton Township, MI*

**Makes about 10 cups of granola**

*Prep. Time: 20 minutes* ⚜ *Cooking Time: 4–6 hours* ⚜ *Ideal slow-cooker size: 6- to 7-qt.*

6 cups old-fashioned oats

¾ cup chopped almonds

½ cup chopped pecans

¾ cup raw sunflower seeds

¼ cup flaxseed

1 cup dried cranberries

1 cup chopped dehydrated apples

1 cup apple butter

¼ cup honey

¼ cup maple syrup

**1.** Place all of the dry ingredients in a bowl and stir.

**2.** Mix together the apple butter, honey, and maple syrup.

**3.** Spray your crock with nonstick spray.

**4.** Pour your granola mixture in the crock with the apple butter mixture on top. Mix thoroughly.

**5.** Cover and cook on Low with the lid vented for 4–6 hours, stirring frequently (every 30–40 minutes) or until the granola is lightly browned and slightly clumpy.

# Welsh Rarebit

*Sharon Timpe, Mequon, WI*

*Makes 6–8 servings*
*Prep. Time: 5 minutes* ❧ *Cooking Time: 1½–2½ hours* ❧ *Ideal slow-cooker size: 4-qt.*

12-oz. can beer
1 Tbsp. dry mustard
1 tsp. Worcestershire sauce
½ tsp. salt
⅛ tsp. black or white pepper
1 lb. American cheese, cubed
1 lb. sharp cheddar cheese, cubed

1. In slow cooker, combine beer, mustard, Worcestershire sauce, salt, and pepper.

2. Cover and cook on High 1–2 hours, until mixture boils.

3. Add cheese, a little at a time, stirring constantly until all the cheese melts.

4. Heat on High 20–30 minutes with cover off, stirring frequently.

Serving suggestion:

Serve hot over toasted English muffins or over toasted bread cut into triangles. Garnish with strips of crisp bacon and tomato slices.

# Blueberry Apple Waffle Topping

*Willard E. Roth, Elkhart, IN*

*Makes 10–12 servings*

*Prep. Time: 10 minutes* ⚶ *Cooking Time: 3 hours* ⚶ *Ideal slow-cooker size: 3½- or 4-qt.*

1 qt. natural applesauce, unsweetened

2 Granny Smith apples, unpeeled, cored, and sliced

1 pt. fresh, or frozen, blueberries

½ Tbsp. ground cinnamon

½ cup pure maple syrup

1 tsp. almond extract

½ cup chopped walnuts

**1.** Stir together applesauce, apples, and blueberries in slow cooker sprayed with nonfat cooking spray.

**2.** Add cinnamon and maple syrup.

**3.** Cover. Cook on Low 3 hours.

**4.** Add almond flavoring and walnuts just before serving.

# Appetizers & Snacks

# Football Party Super Dip

*Colleen Heatwole, Burton, MI*

**Makes 12 minutes**
*Prep. Time: 20 minutes* ⚜ *Cooking Time: 1–2 hours* ⚜ *Ideal slow-cooker size: 2-qt.*

1 lb. ground beef

1 lb. Velveeta® cheese, cubed

8 oz. salsa of choice (mild, medium, or hot)

½ tsp. chili powder

¼ tsp. ground cumin

tortilla chips of choice

**1.** Brown ground beef in a skillet and drain off grease. Crumble into fine pieces and place in slow cooker.

**2.** Place cubed cheese on top.

**3.** Cover. Cook on High 45 minutes or until cheese melts, stirring occasionally.

**4.** Add salsa, chili powder, and cumin.

**5.** Reduce heat to Low and cook until heated through, checking frequently and stirring occasionally.

**6.** Serve with tortilla chips for dipping.

## TIP

This recipe takes a bit more watching than most slow-cooker recipes. You can burn the dip if the slow cooker gets too hot. Use hot or mild salsa, depending on your "heat" preference. You can always add a little hot sauce to your own serving to add a little more heat if you like.

# South of the Border Chicken Dip

*MarJanita Geigley, Lancaster, PA*

**Makes 28 servings**

*Prep. Time: 30 minutes* ⚶ *Cooking Time: 4 hours* ⚶ *Ideal slow-cooker size: 3-qt.*

1 lb. Velveeta® cheese, cubed

10-oz. can diced tomatoes and green chilies, drained

6 oz. chopped and cooked chicken

¼ cup chopped onion

1 tsp. cumin

2 tsp. cilantro

1 dash of Tabasco

1 small jar of salsa

1. Combine all ingredients in slow cooker.

2. Cook on Low for 4 hours.

Serving suggestion:
   Serve with chips and
guacamole.

# Buffalo Chicken Dip

*Amy Troyer, Garden Gove, IA*

*Makes 4–5 servings*
*Prep. Time: 10 minutes* ⚥ *Cooking Time: 2–3 hours* ⚥ *Ideal slow-cooker size: 2-qt.*

8 oz. pkg. cream cheese

1 cup blue cheese or ranch dressing

½ cup Frank's RedHot® Original Cayenne Pepper Sauce

1 cup mozzarella cheese, or your favorite cheese

2 cups cooked and shredded chicken

1. Combine all ingredients in slow cooker.

2. Cover and cook on Low for 2–3 hours.

Serving suggestion:

Serve with tortilla chips.

# Chip Dip

*Janeen Troyer, Fairview, MI*

**Makes 8 servings**
Prep. Time: 20 minutes ☙ Cooking Time: 1½ hours ☙ Ideal slow-cooker size: 2-qt.

1 lb. ground beef or sausage

1 lb. Velveeta cheese, cut into small chunks

your choice of seasonings

milk

1. Brown the beef or sausage on the top of the stove.

2. Pour in a greased crock. Add the cheese and seasonings.

3. Add milk as needed to keep the dip from being too thick.

4. Cover and cook on Low for 1½ hours.

Serving suggestion:
Serve with chips.

# Spicy Chicken & Bean Dip

*Hope Comerford, Clinton Township, MI*

*Makes 10–15 servings*

*Prep. Time: 15 minutes* ☙ *Cooking Time: 4–5 hours* ☙ *Ideal slow-cooker size: 2- to 3-qt.*

1 boneless skinless chicken breast

8-oz. tub low-fat cream cheese with chive & onion, softened

4-oz. can diced green chilies

½ cup diced tomatoes

½ cup diced onion

15-oz. can black beans, drained, rinsed

1 cup shredded Monterey Jack cheese

¼ cup water

2 Tbsp. chili powder

½ tsp. ground cumin

½ tsp. kosher salt

¼ tsp. pepper

1 cup nonfat plain Greek yogurt

1. Place the chicken breast in the crock.

2. In a bowl, mix together the cream cheese, diced green chilies, tomatoes, onion, black beans, cheese, water, chili powder, cumin, salt, and pepper. Pour this mixture over the chicken.

3. Cover and cook on Low for 4–5 hours.

4. When cooking time is up, remove the chicken, shred it, and set aside.

5. In the crock stir in the Greek yogurt, little by little. Mix it well with the beans and sauce. Put the chicken back in the crock and stir for serving.

Serving suggestion:
Serve with baked tortilla chips or celery sticks.

# Refried Bean Dip

*Mabel Shirk, Mount Crawford, VA* ⚬ *Wilma Haberkamp, Fairbank, IA*

**Makes 8–10 servings**

*Prep. Time: 5–10 minutes* ⚬ *Cooking Time: 2–2½ hours* ⚬ *Ideal slow-cooker size: 1- to 2-qt.*

20-oz. can refried beans

1 cup shredded cheddar, or hot pepper, cheese

½ cup chopped green onions

¼ tsp. salt

2–4 Tbsp. bottled taco sauce (depending on your taste preference)

**1.** In slow cooker, combine beans with cheese, onions, salt, and taco sauce.

**2.** Cover and cook on Low 2 to 2½ hours.

Serving suggestion:
Serve hot from the pot with tortilla chips.

# Texas Queso Dip

*Donna Treloar, Muncie, IN* ❧ *Janie Steele, Moore, OK*

**Makes 2 quarts dip**
Prep. Time: 10 minutes ❧ Cooking Time: 2 hours ❧ Ideal slow-cooker size: 4-qt.

1 lb. spicy ground pork sausage, loose

2-lb. block Mexican-style Velveeta cheese, cubed

10-oz. can diced tomatoes with chilies

½ cup milk

**1.** Brown sausage in skillet, breaking it into small chunks as it browns.

**2.** Drain off drippings.

**3.** Combine cheese, tomatoes, and milk in slow cooker.

**4.** Stir in browned sausage.

**5.** Cover and cook 2 hours on Low. Serve while hot.

Serving suggestion:
Serve with tortilla chips.

# Mexican Fiesta Dip

*Hope Comerford, Clinton Township, MI*

*Makes 12–16 servings*
Prep. Time: 15 minutes ⚘ Cooking Time: 2½–3½ hours ⚘ Ideal slow-cooker size: 2-qt.

16-oz. can refried beans
15-oz. can chili with beans
1 clove garlic, minced
1 small onion, chopped
¼ cup jarred sliced jalapeños
4 oz. cream cheese
1 cup shredded Mexican blend cheese

**1.** Spray your crock with nonstick spray.

**2.** Place the refried beans, chili with beans, garlic, onion, and jalapeños into your crock. Stir.

**3.** Cover and cook on Low for 2–3 hours.

**4.** Add the cream cheese and stir until well-mixed.

**5.** Next, add the shredded cheese and stir until well-mixed. Cook an additional 30 minutes or so, or until the cheeses are melted through.

**6.** Switch to Warm.

Serving suggestion:

Serve with tortilla chips.

**TIP**
Depending on the level of spiciness you like, you can add more or less jalapeños to this dip.

# Quick-and-Easy Nacho Dip

Kristina Shull, Timberville, VA

Makes 10–15 servings
Prep. Time: 15 minutes ♣ Cooking Time: 2 hours ♣ Ideal slow-cooker size: 3-qt.

1 lb. ground beef

dash of salt

dash of pepper

dash of onion powder

2 cloves garlic, minced, optional

2 16-oz. jars salsa (as hot or mild as you like)

15-oz. can refried beans

1½ cups sour cream

3 cups shredded cheddar cheese, divided

**1.** Brown ground beef. Drain. Add salt, pepper, onion powder, and minced garlic if you wish.

**2.** Combine beef, salsa, beans, sour cream, and 2 cups cheese in slow cooker.

**3.** Cover. Heat on Low 2 hours. Just before serving, sprinkle with 1 cup cheese.

Serving suggestion:

Serve with tortilla chips.

# Sunday Night Pizza Balls

*MarJanita Geigley, Lancaster, PA*

**Makes 10 servings**
Prep. Time: 15 minutes 🔹 Cooking Time: 2–4 hours 🔹 Ideal slow-cooker size: 7-qt.

3 cans (10 per can) Pillsbury® biscuits
1 jar pizza sauce
60 pepperoni slices
30 cubes of Colby cheese
1 beaten egg
2 cups Parmesan cheese
3 Tbsp. Italian seasoning
2 Tbsp. garlic powder

1. Spray slow cooker with nonstick cooking spray.

2. Flatten out each biscuit.

3. Brush pizza sauce on each one.

4. Put pepperoni and cheese on each biscuit.

5. Gather up edges and tuck together.

6. Brush with egg and place in crock.

7. Sprinkle with Parmesan, Italian seasoning, and garlic powder.

8. Cook on Low for 2–4 hours.

**TIP**
This recipe is a bit labor intensive, but worth the work!

# Sweet 'n' Sour Meatballs

*Valerie Drobel, Carlisle, PA* ❧ *Sharon Hannaby, Frederick, MD*

**Makes 15–20 servings**

*Prep. Time: 10 minutes* ❧ *Cooking Time: 2–4 hours* ❧ *Ideal slow-cooker size: 3- to 4-qt.*

12-oz. jar grape jelly

12-oz. jar chili sauce

2 1-lb. bags prepared frozen meatballs, thawed

**1.** Combine jelly and sauce in slow cooker. Stir well.

**2.** Add meatballs. Stir to coat.

**3.** Cover and heat on Low 4 hours, or on High 2 hours. Keep slow cooker on Low while serving.

**TIP**

If your meatballs are frozen, add another hour to your cook time.

# Meatball Sliders

Hope Comerford, Clinton Township, MI

*Makes 40–50 slider sandwiches, depending on how many meatballs are in your bag*
Prep. Time: 5 minutes  &  Cooking Time: 6–7 hours  &  Ideal slow-cooker size: 6- to 7-qt.

32-oz. bag frozen meatballs, turkey, or beef
14½-oz. can diced chili-ready tomatoes
15-oz. can tomato sauce
2 tsp. garlic powder
2 tsp. dry chopped parsley
Slider buns
Provolone cheese

1. Pour the bag of frozen meatballs into your crock.

2. Pour the diced tomatoes and tomato sauce over the top and sprinkle on the garlic powder and parsley as well.

3. Cover and cook on Low for 6–7 hours.

4. Serve on slider buns with provolone cheese slices.

Serving suggestion:

Serve on a platter with decorative toothpicks in the top of each slider.

**TIP**
Toast the slider buns and let the cheese melt over the top before placing the meatball on the slider.

# Crowd-Pleasing Rib Tips

*Hope Comerford, Clinton Township, MI*

*Makes 4–6 servings*
*Prep. Time: 5 minutes* ⚓ *Cooking Time: 8 hours* ⚓ *Ideal slow-cooker size: 5-qt.*

3–4 lbs. rib tips

**Rub:**

⅓ cup brown sugar

1 tsp. kosher salt

1 tsp. chili powder

1 tsp. onion powder

1 tsp. garlic powder

½ tsp. cayenne pepper

8 oz. barbecue sauce (your favorite)

1. Spray crock with nonstick spray.

2. Place rib tips in crock.

3. Mix together the rub ingredients. Rub this into all of the rib tips in the crock.

4. Pour the barbecue sauce over the rib tips.

5. Cover and cook on Low for 8 hours.

# Mini Hot Dogs and Meatballs

*Mary Kay Nolt, Newmanstown, PA*

**Makes 15 servings**
*Prep. Time: 5 minutes*   ⚮   *Cooking Time: 2–3 hours*   ⚮   *Ideal slow-cooker size: 5- to 6-qt.*

36 frozen cooked Italian meatballs (½-oz. each)

16-oz. pkg. miniature hot dogs, or little smoked sausages

26-oz. jar meatless spaghetti sauce

18-oz. bottle barbecue sauce

12-oz. bottle chili sauce

**1.** Combine all ingredients in slow cooker.

**2.** Cover and cook on High for 2 hours, or on Low for 3 hours, until heated through.

# Slow-Cooked Smokies

*Renee Baum, Chambersburg, PA*

**Makes 12–16 servings**
*Prep. Time: 5 minutes* ⚶ *Cooking Time: 6–7 hours* ⚶ *Ideal slow-cooker size: 3- to 4-qt.*

2 lbs. miniature smoked sausage links

28-oz. bottle barbecue sauce

1 ¼ cups water

3 Tbsp. Worcestershire sauce

3 Tbsp. steak sauce

½ tsp. pepper

**1.** In a slow cooker, combine all ingredients. Mix well.

**2.** Cover and cook on Low 6–7 hours.

# Bourbon Dogs

*Lois Ostrander, Lebanon, PA*

**Makes 20 servings**

*Prep. Time: 10 minutes*    *Cooking Time: 4 hours*    *Ideal slow-cooker size: 3-qt.*

4 cups ketchup

1 ½ cups brown sugar

1 ½ cups bourbon whiskey

2 Tbsp. chopped onion

½ cup water

3-lb. pkg. miniature smoked sausage links

**1.** Combine ketchup, brown sugar, bourbon, onion, and water in slow cooker. Cook on High for 2 hours.

**2.** Gently stir in sausages and cook on Low for an additional 4 hours.

**TIP**

This makes a great appetizer for any meal, but it is a real success at a buffet or tailgate party.

# Kielbasa Bites

*Shelia Heil, Lancaster, PA*

**Makes 6 servings**
*Prep. Time: 5 minutes* ☙ *Cooking Time: 2–3 hours* ☙ *Ideal slow-cooker size: 4- to 5-qt.*

12-oz. kielbasa ring, sliced on the bias
in ¼-inch slices

12-oz. can cola

⅓ cup brown sugar

**1.** Combine kielbasa slices, cola, and brown sugar in slow cooker.

**2.** Cover and cook on Low for 2–3 hours, stirring several times. Cook until thickened.

**3.** Serve with toothpicks.

**TIP**
May also be used as a sauce over rice or pasta for a meal instead of an appetizer.

# Apricot-Glazed Wings

*Hope Comerford, Clinton Township, MI*

**Makes 8–10 servings**
*Prep. Time: 30 minutes   ❧   Broiling Time: 16 minutes   ❧   Cooking Time: 4–6 hours*
*❧   Ideal slow-cooker size: 3-qt.*

4 lbs. chicken wings, cut at the joint, tips removed and discarded

salt, to taste

pepper, to taste

garlic powder, to taste

12-oz. jar apricot preserves

¼ cup honey Catalina dressing

2 Tbsp. honey mustard

2 Tbsp. barbecue sauce

1 tsp. lime juice

4 dashes hot sauce

1 small onion, minced

**1.** Preheat your oven to a low broil.

**2.** Put your wing pieces onto a baking sheet and sprinkle both sides with salt, pepper, and garlic powder. Put them under the broiler for 8 minutes on each side.

**3.** While the wings are broiling, mix together the apricot preserves, honey Catalina dressing, honey mustard, barbecue sauce, lime juice, hot sauce, and onion.

**4.** When your wings are done under the broiler, place them into a greased crock.

**5.** Pour the sauce you just mixed over the top, then use tongs to toss the wings around to make sure they're all coated with the sauce.

**6.** Cook on Low for 4–6 hours.

**TIP**
Serve with fresh celery sticks.

# Sweet Barbecue Wings

*Hope Comerford, Clinton Township, MI*

**Makes 6–8 servings**
Prep. Time: 20 minutes   ⚜   Broiling Time: 16 minutes   ⚜   Cooking Time: 4–5 hours
⚜   Ideal slow-cooker size: 2-qt.

3 lbs. chicken wings, wing tips cut off and discarded, cut at the joint

salt, to taste

pepper, to taste

garlic powder, to taste

12-oz. jar orange marmalade

½ cup barbecue sauce

2 Tbsp. quick-cooking tapioca

1 Tbsp. Dijon mustard

**1.** Preheat your oven to a low broil.

**2.** Put the wing pieces onto a baking sheet and sprinkle both sides with salt, pepper, and garlic powder. Put them under the broiler for 8 minutes on each side.

**3.** While the wings are broiling, mix together the orange marmalade, barbecue sauce, tapioca, and Dijon mustard in a small bowl.

**4.** When wings are browned, transfer them to your greased crock.

**5.** Pour the sauce over the chicken and use tongs to mix them through the sauce.

**6.** Cover and cook on Low for 4–5 hours.

# Jalapeño Poppers

*Amanda Gross, Souderton, PA*

**Makes 10 servings**
*Prep. Time: 10 minutes* ❧ *Cooking Time: 2–3 hours* ❧ *Ideal slow-cooker size: 5½-qt.*

10 medium jalapeños

4 oz. cream cheese, room temperature

¼ cup sour cream, room temperature

9 slices bacon, cooked and crumbled

¼ tsp. garlic salt

⅓ cup water

**1.** Cut off the tops and remove seeds and membranes to hollow out jalapeños.

**2.** In a bowl, mix together cream cheese, sour cream, bacon, and garlic salt.

**3.** Gently stuff cheese mixture into peppers.

**4.** Put water in the bottom of the slow cooker. Place peppers on top.

**5.** Cover and cook on High 2–3 hours, until peppers look slightly wrinkly and wilted.

## TIP

Wear gloves to prepare the jalapeños if you are sensitive to the burning oils in hot peppers.

# Game Day Snack Mix

*Hope Comerford, Clinton Township, MI*

**Makes 8 cups**

Prep. Time: 15 minutes  &  Cooking Time: 2 hours  &  Cooling Time: 3 hours  &  Ideal slow-cooker size: 6-qt.

3 cups Rice Chex®

3 cups Corn Chex®

1 cup pretzel sticks

1 cup dried cranberries

1 cup raisins

1 cup unsalted cashews

1 cup unsalted peanuts

½ cup butter

½ cup maple syrup

1 Tbsp. vanilla extract

1 tsp. salt

1 tsp. cinnamon

**1.** Spray crock with nonstick spray.

**2.** Place Rice Chex, Corn Chex, pretzels, cranberries, raisins, cashews, and peanuts in crock.

**3.** In a microwave-safe bowl, melt the butter. Mix the butter with the maple syrup, vanilla, salt, and cinnamon. Pour this mixture over the contents of the crock and stir gently with a rubber spatula until all contents are well-coated.

**4.** Cover and cook on High for about 2 hours, stirring every 20 minutes.

**5.** Pour snack mix onto parchment paper and spread it out. Let it cool for about 3 hours. Store in an airtight container for about 5 days.

**TIP**

Change up the cereal if you prefer something a bit different to snack on.

# Chili Nuts

*Barbara Aston, Ashdown, AR*

*Makes 5 cups nuts*

*Prep. Time: 5 minutes* ⚓ *Cooking Time: 2–2¾ hours* ⚓ *Ideal slow-cooker size: 3-qt.*

¼ cup melted butter

2 12-oz. cans cocktail peanuts

1⅝-oz. pkg. chili seasoning mix

**1.** Pour butter over nuts in slow cooker. Sprinkle in dry chili mix. Toss together.

**2.** Cover. Heat on Low 2–2½ hours. Turn to High. Remove lid and cook 10–15 minutes.

# All-American Snack

Doris M. Coyle-Zipp, South Ozone Park, NY  &  Melissa Raber, Millersburg, OH
&  Ada Miller, Sugarcreek, OH  &  Nanci Keatley, Salem, OR

*Makes 3 quarts snack mix*
Prep. Time: 10 minutes  &  Cooking Time: 3 hours  &  Ideal slow-cooker size: 4-qt.

3 cups thin pretzel sticks
4 cups Wheat Chex®
4 cups Cheerios®
12-oz. can salted peanuts
4 Tbsp. melted butter, or margarine
1 tsp. garlic powder
1 tsp. celery salt
½ tsp. seasoned salt
2 Tbsp. grated Parmesan cheese

**1.** Combine pretzels, cereal, and peanuts in large bowl.

**2.** Melt butter. Stir in garlic powder, celery salt, seasoned salt, and Parmesan cheese. Pour over pretzels, cereal, and peanuts. Toss until well mixed.

**3.** Pour into slow cooker. Cover. Cook on Low 2½ hours, stirring every 30 minutes. Remove lid and cook another 30 minutes on Low.

# Spiced Mixed Nuts

*Sharon Wantland, Menomonee Falls, WI*

*Makes 12–16 servings*

*Prep. Time: 15 minutes* & *Cooking Time: 2 hours* & *Ideal slow-cooker size: 3-qt.*

1 egg white

2 tsp. vanilla extract

1 cup almonds

1 cup pecan halves

1 cup walnuts

1 cup unsalted cashews

1 cup sugar

1 cup packed brown sugar

4 tsp. ground cinnamon

2 tsp. ground ginger

1 tsp. ground nutmeg

½ tsp. ground cloves

⅛ tsp. salt

2 Tbsp. water

1. In a large bowl, whisk egg white and vanilla together until blended.

2. Stir in nuts until well-coated.

3. In a small bowl, mix sugars, spices, and salt together.

4. Add to nut mixture and toss to coat.

5. Transfer mixture to slow cooker. Cover and cook nuts on High for 1½ hours, stirring every 15 minutes.

6. Sprinkle in water, stirring gently.

7. Cook covered on Low 20–30 more minutes.

8. Spread onto waxed paper and let cool. Store in airtight container up to 1 week.

# Soups, Stews & Chilies

# Creamy Potato Soup

*Hope Comerford, Clinton Township, MI*

**Makes 6 servings**
*Prep. Time: 20 minutes* ⚬ *Cooking Time: 8–10 hours* ⚬ *Ideal slow-cooker size: 5-qt.*

8–9 Idaho potatoes, chopped into bite-sized pieces

10¾-oz. can cream of chicken soup

4 cups chicken broth or stock

1 medium onion, chopped

2–4 carrots, chopped

1–2 stalks celery, chopped

3 green onions, chopped

8-oz. block cream cheese, chopped into cubes

¼ cup sour cream

2 tsp. garlic powder

1 tsp. onion powder

1½ tsp. pepper

1 tsp. salt

1. Place all ingredients into your crock and stir.
2. Cook on Low for 8–10 hours.

Serving suggestion:
Serve with fresh chopped chives or green onions on top and little bit of shredded cheese.

**TIP**
Use an immersion blender to give your soup a smoother and creamier texture.

# Slow-Cooker Loaded Baked Potato Soup

*Becky Fixel, Grosse Pointe Farms, MI*

**Makes 8–10 servings**

*Prep. Time: 15 minutes  &  Cooking Time: 6 hours  &  Ideal slow-cooker size: 5-qt.*

32 oz. chicken broth

2 cups heavy cream

5–7 medium potatoes, cubed

1 small onion, chopped

**1.** Empty the broth and cream into your crock.

**2.** Add the chopped potatoes and onion. Stir until combined.

**3.** Cover and cook on High for 6 hours.

**4.** With an immersion blender or a potato masher mash any remaining chunks in your soup.

Serving suggestion:

Top with shredded cheese, cooked chopped bacon, and chopped green onions.

# Easy Potato Soup

*Yvonne Kauffman, Boettger Harrisonburg, VA*

*Makes 8 servings*
*Prep. Time: 10 minutes ♣ Cooking Time: 5 hours ♣ Ideal slow-cooker size: 4- to 6-qt.*

3 cups chicken broth
2-lb. bag frozen hash brown potatoes
1½ tsp. salt
¾ tsp. pepper
3 cups milk
3 cups shredded Monterey Jack or cheddar cheese

**1.** Place chicken broth, potatoes, salt, and pepper in slow cooker.

**2.** Cover and cook on High 4 hours, or until potatoes are soft.

**3.** Leaving the broth and potatoes in the slow cooker, mash the potatoes lightly, leaving some larger chunks.

**4.** Add milk and cheese. Blend in thoroughly.

**5.** Cover and cook on High until cheese melts and soup is hot.

# Velveeta Cheese Soup

*Colleen Heatwole, Burton, MI*

*Makes 6–8 servings*
Prep. Time: 20 minutes   ⚬   Cooking Time: 4–6 hours   ⚬   Ideal slow-cooker size: 6-qt.

1 lb. ground beef

1 medium onion, chopped finely

1 lb. Velveeta cheese (can use store brand), cubed

15- or 15¼-oz. can corn, undrained

15-oz. can kidney beans, undrained

15-oz. can black beans, undrained

30- to 32-oz. canned tomatoes

2 Tbsp. dry taco seasoning mix

**1.** Brown beef with onion. Drain.

**2.** Combine all ingredients and add along with beef and onion to slow cooker.

**3.** Cover and cook on Low 4–6 hours.

Serving suggestion:
  Serve with corn chips, grated cheese, and dollops of sour cream.

**TIP**
It always helps to spray your slow cooker with vegetable cooking spray before adding ingredients.

# French Onion Soup

*Hope Comerford, Clinton Township, MI*

**Makes 6–8 servings**
Prep. Time: 10 minutes  &  Cooking Time: 7–8 hours  &  Ideal slow-cooker size: 5-qt.

3–4 large sweet yellow onions, sliced thinly

½ tsp. pepper

1 bay leaf

2 sprigs fresh thyme

7 cups beef stock

1 cup dry white wine (such as a Chardonnay)

loaf of French bread, sliced

4 oz. Gruyère cheese, sliced thinly

**1.** Place all of the onions into the crock and sprinkle them with the pepper. Add the bay leaf and sprigs of thyme.

**2.** Pour in the beef stock and wine.

**3.** Cover and cook on Low for 7–8 hours. Remove the thyme sprigs and bay leaf.

**4.** Serve each bowl of soup in an oven-safe bowl and place a slice of bread on top, topped with enough cheese to cover the entire top. Place it in the oven under the broiler for a few minutes, or until the cheese starts to bubble.

# Split Pea Soup

*Phyllis Good, Lancaster, PA*

*Makes 8–10 servings*
*Prep. Time: 20 minutes* ⚜ *Cooking Time: 4–8 hours* ⚜ *Ideal slow-cooker size: 6-qt.*

3 cups dried split peas (a little over 1 pound)

3 quarts water

½ tsp. garlic powder

½ tsp. dried oregano

1 cup of diced, or thinly sliced, carrots

1 cup chopped celery

1 tsp. salt

¼–½ tsp. pepper (coarsely ground is great)

1 ham shank or hock

**1.** Put all ingredients into slow cooker, except the ham. Stir well.

**2.** Settle ham into mixture.

**3.** Cover. Cook on Low 4–8 hours, or until ham is tender and falling off the bone, and the peas are very soft.

**4.** Use a slotted spoon to lift the ham bone out of the soup. Allow it to cool until you can handle it without burning yourself.

**5.** Cut the ham into bite-sized pieces. Stir it back into the soup.

**6.** Heat the soup for 10 minutes, and then serve.

# Black Bean and Ham Soup

*Colleen Heatwole, Burton, MI*

**Makes 4 servings**
Prep. Time: 30 minutes   ♣   Cooking Time: 6–8 hours   ♣   Ideal slow-cooker size: 5-qt.

2 cups chopped carrots

1 cup chopped celery

2 cloves garlic, minced

1 medium onion, chopped

2 15½-oz. cans black beans, undrained

2 14½-oz. cans chicken or vegetable broth

15-oz. can crushed tomatoes

1½ tsp. dried basil

½ tsp. dried oregano

½ tsp. ground cumin

½ tsp. chili powder

¼ tsp. hot pepper sauce

1 cup diced cooked ham

1. Combine all ingredients in slow cooker.

2. Cover and cook on Low 6–8 hours or until vegetables are tender.

# Ham and Beans

*Jenny R. Unternahrer, Wayland, IA*

**Makes 6–8 servings**
*Prep. Time: 10 minutes* ⚶ *Cooking Time: 6–8 hours* ⚶ *Ideal slow-cooker size: 6-qt.*

1 lb. bag dried great northern beans

Leftover ham chunk (approx. 1–2 lbs.)

6 cups water, or chicken or vegetable broth

1½ Tbsp. minced garlic

1 medium onion, chopped

½ tsp. salt

**1.** Sort through your beans to make sure there aren't any rocks (yes, sometimes they make it through processing) or any odd looking beans. Rinse. Place beans and rest of the ingredients in the slow cooker.

**2.** Cover and cook on Low for 6–8 hours, or until beans are tender.

**3.** Shred the ham a little so everyone gets both beans and ham in their bowl.

*Serving suggestion:*
*Great served with a slice of cornbread.*

**TIP**
This recipe does great doubled. Just cook for approximately 12 hours on Low.

# Shredded Pork Tortilla Soup

*Hope Comerford, Clinton Township, MI*

**Makes 6–8 servings**

*Prep. Time: 10 minutes* ⚖ *Cooking Time: 8–10 hours* ⚖ *Ideal slow-cooker size: 5-qt.*

3 large tomatoes, chopped

1 cup chopped red onion

1 jalapeño, seeded and minced

1 lb. pork loin

2 tsp. cumin

2 tsp. chili powder

2 tsp. onion powder

2 tsp. garlic powder

2 tsp. lime juice

8 cups chicken broth

**garnish (optional):**

fresh chopped cilantro

tortilla chips

avocado slices

freshly grated Mexican cheese

**1.** In your crock, place the tomatoes, onion, and jalapeños.

**2.** Place the pork loin on top.

**3.** Add all the seasonings and lime juice, and pour in the chicken broth.

**4.** Cover and cook on Low for 8–10 hours.

**5.** Remove the pork and shred it between two forks. Place it back into the soup and stir.

**6.** Serve each bowl of soup with fresh chopped cilantro, tortilla chips, avocado slices and freshly grated Mexican cheese, if desired . . . or any other garnishes you would like!

## TIP

If you don't have time for freshly chopped tomatoes, use a can of diced or chopped tomatoes.

# Taco Soup

*Hope Comerford, Clinton Township, MI*

**Makes 4–6 servings**
Prep. Time: 20 minutes  &  Cooking Time: 8 hours  &  Ideal slow-cooker size: 4-qt.

1 lb. ground turkey

1 large onion, chopped

salt, to taste

pepper, to taste

1-oz. pkg. ranch dressing/seasoning mix

1 pkg. taco seasoning

1 tsp. cumin

1 tsp. garlic powder

1 cup pinto beans

15½-oz. can chili beans

1 cup frozen whole kernel corn

2 14½-oz. cans diced tomatoes (chili flavor)

4 cups beef broth or stock

**1.** Brown turkey meat with the onion, salt, and pepper.

**2.** Place the browned meat into the crock and add all the remaining ingredients. Stir.

**3.** Cover and cook on Low for 8 hours.

Serving suggestion:
Serve with sour cream, cheese, and tortilla chips.

**TIP**
This recipe does great doubled.

# Southwest Chicken and White Bean Soup

*Karen Ceneviva, Seymour, CT*

**Makes 6 servings**

*Prep. Time: 15 minutes* ⚜ *Cooking Time: 4–10 hours* ⚜ *Ideal slow-cooker size: 3½-qt.*

1 Tbsp. vegetable oil

1 lb. boneless, skinless chicken breasts, cut into 1-inch cubes

1¾ cups chicken broth

1 cup chunky salsa

3 cloves garlic, minced

2 Tbsp. cumin

15½-oz. can small white beans, drained and rinsed

1 cup frozen corn

1 large onion, chopped

**1.** Heat oil in 10-inch skillet over medium to high heat. Add chicken and cook until it is well browned on all sides. Stir frequently to prevent sticking.

**2.** Mix broth, salsa, garlic, cumin, beans, corn, and onion in slow cooker. Add chicken. Stir well.

**3.** Cover. Cook 8–10 hours on Low or 4–5 hours on High.

# Buffalo Chicken Wing Soup

Mary Lynn Miller, Reinholds, PA ⚶ Donna Neiter, Wausau, WI
⚶ Joette Droz, Kalona, IA

*Makes 8 servings*
*Prep. Time: 10 minutes ⚶ Cooking Time: 4–5 hours ⚶ Ideal slow-cooker size: 3-qt.*

6 cups milk

3 10¾-oz. cans condensed cream of chicken soup, undiluted

3 cups (about 1 lb.) shredded or cubed cooked chicken

1 cup (8 ozs.) sour cream

1–8 Tbsp. hot pepper sauce, according to your preference for heat!

**1.** Combine milk and soups in slow cooker until smooth.

**2.** Stir in chicken.

**3.** Cover and cook on Low 3¾–4¾ hours.

**4.** Fifteen minutes before serving stir in sour cream and hot sauce.

**5.** Cover and continue cooking just until bubbly.

# Steak and Wild Rice Soup

*Sally Holzem, Schofield, WI*

*Makes 6 servings*

*Prep. Time: 15 minutes  ☙  Cooking Time: 5 hours  ☙  Ideal slow-cooker size: 5-qt.*

4 cups beef stock

3 cups cubed, cooked roast beef

4 oz. sliced fresh mushrooms

½ cup chopped onion

¼ cup ketchup

2 tsp. apple cider vinegar

I tsp. brown sugar

I tsp. Worcestershire sauce

⅛ tsp. ground mustard

1½ cups cooked wild rice

I cup frozen peas

**1.** Combine stock, beef, mushrooms, onion, ketchup, vinegar, sugar, Worcestershire sauce, and mustard in slow cooker.

**2.** Cook on Low 4 hours.

**3.** Add rice and peas. Cook an additional hour on Low.

**TIP**

Great way to use up scraps of meat and broth left from a roast beef, and a nice way to transform leftover wild rice.

# Scotch Broth

*Jean Turner, Williams Lake, BC*

*Makes 6–8 servings*
*Prep. Time: 15 minutes* ⚜ *Cooking Time: 3–4 hours* ⚜ *Ideal slow-cooker size: 4-qt.*

2 lbs. lamb shoulder meat, chopped

6 cups water

1 large onion, chopped

1 cup chopped celery

1 cup diced carrots

⅓ cup pearl barley

½ cup yellow or green split peas, rinsed and picked over

1 tsp. salt

¼ tsp. ground black pepper

1 bay leaf

3 Tbsp. chopped fresh parsley

**1.** Combine all ingredients in slow cooker except parsley.

**2.** Cover and cook on High for 3–4 hours, until meat is tender and split peas are done.

**3.** Stir in parsley. Remove bay leaf before serving.

Variation:

Beef can be used in place of lamb.

**TIP**
Great with garlic bread for supper on a cold night.

# Kielbasa Soup

*Bernice M. Gnidovec, Streator, IL*

**Makes 8 servings**
*Prep. Time: 10 minutes* ⚜ *Cooking Time: 12 hours* ⚜ *Ideal slow-cooker size: 8-qt.*

16-oz. pkg. frozen mixed vegetables, or your choice of vegetables

6-oz. can tomato paste

1 medium onion, chopped

3 medium potatoes, diced

1½ lbs. kielbasa, cut into ¼-inch pieces

4 qts. water

1. Combine all ingredients in large slow cooker.

2. Cover. Cook on Low 12 hours.

# Shrimp Soup/Chowder

*Joanne Good, Wheaton, IL*

**Makes 12 servings**
Prep. Time: 25 minutes    Cooking Time: 7 hours    Ideal slow-cooker size: 4-qt.

1 medium onion, chopped

5 medium russet potatoes, peeled and cubed

1½ cups diced, pre-cooked ham

4–6 cups water

salt and pepper, to taste

2 lbs. shrimp, peeled, deveined, and cooked

**chowder option:**

4 Tbsp. flour

1 cup heavy (whipping) cream

**1.** Place chopped onion in microwave-safe bowl and cook in microwave for 2 minutes on High.

**2.** Place onion, cubed potatoes, diced ham, and 4 cups water in slow cooker. (If you're making the chowder option, whisk 4 Tbsp. flour into the 4 cups water in bowl before adding to slow cooker.)

**3.** Cover and cook on Low for 7 hours, or until potatoes are softened. If soup base is thicker than you like, add up to 2 cups more water.

**4.** About 15–20 minutes before serving, turn heat to High and add shrimp. If making chowder, also add heavy cream. Cook until shrimp are hot, about 15 minutes.

Variation:

To be added in Step 2: ½ tsp. thyme and 1 bay leaf (remove bay leaf before serving).

# Chet's Trucker Stew

*Janice Muller, Derwood, MD*

**Makes 10 servings**
*Prep. Time: 30 minutes* ⚜ *Cooking Time: 3–4 hours* ⚜ *Ideal slow-cooker size: 5-qt.*

1 lb. cooked Jimmy Dean's® sausage, drained and crumbled

1 can wax beans, drained

1 can lima beans, drained

1 lb. cooked ground meat, drained

1 cup ketchup

27-oz. can pork & beans with juice

1 cup brown sugar

1 can light kidney beans with juice

1 can dark kidney beans with juice

1 Tbsp. Gulden's® Spicy Brown mustard

1. Combine all ingredients in slow cooker.

2. Cover and cook on High for 3–4 hours.

Serving suggestion:
This pairs well with cornbread or a loaf of warm Italian bread.

# "Absent Cook" Stew

Kathy Hertzler, Lancaster, PA

Makes 5–6 servings
Prep. Time: 15 minutes ⚭ Cooking Time: 10–12 hours ⚭ Ideal slow-cooker size: 3- to 4-qt.

2 lbs. stewing beef, cubed
2–3 carrots, sliced
1 onion, chopped
3 large potatoes, cubed
3 ribs celery, sliced
10¾-oz. can tomato soup
1 soup can water
1 tsp. salt
dash of pepper
2 Tbsp. vinegar

1. Combine all ingredients in slow cooker.

2. Cover. Cook on Low 10–12 hours.

# Pirate Stew

*Nancy Graves, Manhattan, KS*

*Makes 4–6 servings*
Prep. Time: 15 minutes   ⚬   Cooking Time: 6 hours   ⚬   Ideal slow-cooker size: 4-qt.

¾ cup sliced onion

1 lb. ground beef

¼ cup uncooked, long-grain rice

3 cups diced raw potatoes

1 cup diced celery

2 cups canned kidney beans, drained

1 tsp. salt

⅛ tsp. pepper

¼ tsp. chili powder

¼ tsp. Worcestershire sauce

1 cup tomato sauce

½ cup water

**1.** Brown onions and ground beef in skillet. Drain.

**2.** Layer ingredients in slow cooker in order given.

**3.** Cover. Cook on Low 6 hours, or until potatoes and rice are cooked.

# Campfire Stew

*Sharon Wantland, Menomonee Falls, WI*

*Makes 4 servings*
*Prep. Time: 15 minutes  &  Cooking Time: 2–3 hours  &  Ideal slow-cooker size: 2-qt.*

1 lb. ground beef
1 medium onion, chopped
half a green pepper, chopped
salt and pepper, to taste
2 cans vegetable soup, your favorite variety

**1.** Brown ground beef with onions and green pepper in a nonstick skillet, stirring until crumbly. Drain.

**2.** Combine all ingredients in slow cooker.

**3.** Cover and cook on Low 2–3 hours.

# Quick Sausage Stew

*Beverly Hummel, Fleetwood, PA*

**Makes 10 servings**
*Prep. Time: 20 minutes  ⚜  Cooking Time: 4–5 hours  ⚜  Ideal slow-cooker size: 7-qt.*

2 Tbsp. beef bouillon

2 cups water

1 lb. fresh or Italian sausage, sliced thin

½ cup chopped onion

½ cup chopped bell pepper

1-lb. bag frozen carrots

1-lb. bag frozen green beans

4 medium potatoes, cubed

24-oz. can spaghetti sauce

salt and pepper, to taste

1 Tbsp. Worcestershire sauce

**1.** Dissolve beef bouillon in the 2 cups water.

**2.** Brown sausage in skillet. Transfer to slow cooker.

**3.** Pour in bouillon/water and rest of ingredients.

**4.** Cover and cook on Low for 4–5 hours.

**TIP**
This is a hearty soup, a great way to feed a large group. You may substitute ground beef for the sausage.

# Gumbo

*Dorothy Ealy, Los Angeles, CA*

**Makes 8 servings**

Prep. Time: 30 minutes   ⚘   Cooking Time: 4½–5½ hours   ⚘   Ideal slow-cooker size: 5-qt.

2 onions, chopped

3 ribs celery, chopped

½ cup diced green bell pepper

2 cloves garlic, chopped

1 cup chopped fresh or frozen okra

½ cup diced andouille or chorizo sausage

2 15-oz. cans tomatoes, undrained

3 Tbsp. tomato paste

1 chicken bouillon cube

¼ tsp. freshly ground black pepper

¼ tsp. dried thyme

1½ lbs. raw shrimp, peeled and deveined, chopped if large

**1.** In slow cooker, combine onions, celery, bell pepper, garlic, okra, sausage, tomatoes, tomato paste, bouillon cube, black pepper, and thyme.

**2.** Cover and cook on Low for 4–5 hours, until vegetables are soft.

**3.** Add shrimp. Cook for 15–20 more minutes on Low, until shrimp are just opaque and cooked through. Thin gumbo if necessary with a little water, broth, or wine. Taste and adjust salt.

## TIPS

Serve over rice, or serve with French bread. Pass the hot sauce so people can make it really authentically spicy! If you are peeling the shrimp yourself, save the shells. Place them in a saucepan with water or chicken broth just to cover and simmer for 30 minutes. Strain out shells and discard. This makes a tasty seafood-infused broth for making other soups or thinning the gumbo.

# Beer Chili

*Hope Comerford, Clinton Township, MI*

**Makes 4–6 servings**
*Prep. Time: 20 minutes  &  Cooking Time: 7–8 hours  &  Ideal slow-cooker size: 5-qt.*

½ lb. ground beef, browned

15¼-oz. can of black beans, drained, rinsed

14½-oz. can of diced tomatoes with green chilies

4-oz. can tomato sauce

12 oz. beer

1 large onion, chopped

1 beef bouillon cube

1 Tbsp. garlic powder

1 tsp. cumin

1 tsp. chili powder

1. Place all of the ingredients into the crock and stir.

2. Cover and cook on Low for 7–8 hours.

Serving suggestion:
Serve with corn muffins or crackers.

**TIP**

If you like a more "hearty" chili, add more ground beef. For more spice, increase the cumin, or add a 4 oz. can of diced green chilies.

# Bison Chili

*Willard E. Roth, Elkhart, IN*

**Makes 12 servings**
*Prep. Time: 20 minutes* ❧ *Cooking Time: 3–5 hours* ❧ *Ideal slow-cooker size: 7-qt.*

1½ lbs. ground bison

1 Tbsp. olive oil

1 tsp. ground cumin

1 Tbsp. chili powder

1 tsp. powdered garlic

1½ cups chopped onion

1 cup port, *divided*

4 15-oz. cans red kidney beans, *divided*

3 15-oz. cans diced tomatoes

⅓ cup dark brown sugar

4 1-oz. squares unsweetened baking chocolate (100% cacao)

**1.** In skillet, brown bison in oil with cumin, chili powder, garlic, onion, and ½ cup port for 15 minutes. Stir frequently, breaking up the meat into small chunks.

**2.** Spray slow cooker with cooking spray. Turn on High. Put in 3 cans of beans with juice. Add meat mixture.

**3.** Stir in tomatoes and brown sugar.

**4.** In same skillet, melt baking chocolate, watching carefully so it doesn't burn.

**5.** Stir in remaining can of beans and juice. Add to slow-cooker mixture.

**6.** Over medium heat, stir in remaining port, stirring up browned bits from skillet with a wooden spoon. When they're all loosened, add to slow cooker.

**7.** Cook on High for 3 hours, or Low for 5 hours.

Variation:

You can substitute ground beef (or venison) for the bison and have a wonderfully tasty dish!

# Comerford-Style Chili

*Hope Comerford, Clinton Township, MI*

*Makes 4–6 servings*
*Prep. Time: 20 minutes  &  Cooking Time: 7–8 hours  &  Ideal slow-cooker size: 3-qt.*

1 lb. ground round, browned and grease drained

1 medium onion, chopped

15½-oz. can kidney beans

2 14½-oz. cans diced tomatoes

10¾-oz. can Campbell's tomato soup

1 beef bouillon cube

2 cloves garlic, minced

1 tsp. salt

1 tsp. pepper

2 tsp. tarragon

1 tsp. chili powder

Water (how much will depend on how thick or soupy you like your chili)

1. Add all ingredients to your crock.

2. Cover and cook on Low for 7–8 hours.

**TIP**
Can be served with shredded cheddar cheese and sour cream.

# Main Dishes

# Slow-Cooker Beef Stroganoff

*Becky Fixel, Grosse Pointe Farms, MI*

*Makes 6–8 servings*
*Prep. Time: 10 minutes  ♣  Cooking Time: 6 hours  ♣  Ideal slow-cooker size: 5-qt.*

1 cup sour cream
8 oz. cream cheese
¼ cup gluten-free condensed mushroom soup mix
1 medium onion, minced
¼ cup butter
1 lb. stew beef
⅛ tsp. paprika
8–10 oz. mushrooms, sliced
½ cup milk
1 tsp. salt
1 tsp. pepper

1. Mix sour cream, cream cheese, and mushroom soup in medium bowl.

2. Add all ingredients to your crock and mix well.

3. Cover and cook on Low for 6 hours. You may stir occasionally.

# Dutch Steak

*Jane Geigley, Lancaster, PA*

**Makes 6 servings**
Prep. Time: 30 minutes ❧ Cooking Time: 4–6 hours ❧ Ideal slow-cooker size: 5-qt.

1 cup fine cracker crumbs
1 cup cold milk
3 lbs. hamburger
salt and pepper, to taste
2 cup flour
1 Tbsp. butter
10¾-oz. can cream of mushroom soup

**1.** Mix crackers and milk in dish.

**2.** Mix in hamburger and salt and pepper.

**3.** Pat in flat dish and set in fridge overnight.

**4.** Cut into 6 portions.

**5.** Roll in flour and brown both sides in saucepan with butter.

**6.** Put in crock and pour can of cream of mushroom soup over the top.

**7.** Cover and cook on Low for 4–6 hours.

Serving suggestion:
Pairs well with mashed potatoes.

# Slow-Cooker Sirloin Steak

*Amy Troyer, Garden Grove, IA*

**Makes 4–5 servings**
Prep. Time: 10 minutes  ❧  Cooking Time: 6–8 hours  ❧  Ideal slow-cooker size: 2- to 3-qt.

2½-lb. sirloin steak, cut into ½-inch strips
1 large onion, sliced
2 bell peppers, sliced
1 tsp. ginger
1 Tbsp. sugar
2 Tbsp. oil
½ cup soy sauce
2 cloves garlic, minced

1. Place steak in slow cooker, and top with the sliced onion and peppers.

2. Mix together remaining ingredients.

3. Pour sauce over meat, onions, and peppers.

4. Cook on Low 6–8 hours.

Serving suggestion:
    Serve in fresh tortillas with sour cream and sautéed peppers and onions.

# Pot Roast

*Judith Martin, Lebanon, PA*

**Makes 12–15 servings**
*Prep. Time: 5 minutes* ❧ *Cooking Time: 7–8 hours* ❧ *Ideal slow-cooker size: 4-qt.*

2 2½-lb. boneless beef chuck roasts
1 envelope ranch salad dressing mix
1 envelope Italian salad dressing mix
1 envelope brown gravy mix
½–1 cup water

1. Place chuck roasts in a slow cooker.

2. Combine rest of ingredients and pour over the roasts.

3. Cover and cook on low for 7–8 hours.

Serving suggestion:
 Turn the juice into a nice gravy. This roast is very good reheated and served over potatoes with the gravy.

# Chuck Roast

*Janie Steele, Moore, OK*

*Makes 6–8 servings*
*Prep. Time: 20 minutes* ❧ *Cooking Time: 8 hours* ❧ *Ideal slow-cooker size: 5-qt.*

¼ cup flour

salt and pepper, to taste

3–4 pound boneless chuck roast

3 Tbsp. canola oil

4 Tbsp. butter

10 pepperoncini, fresh or jarred

2 Tbsp. mayonnaise

2 tsp. apple cider vinegar

¼ tsp. dried dill

⅛ tsp. paprika

**1.** Mix flour, salt, and pepper and rub into roast. Brown in canola oil. Place roast in crock.

**2.** Top with butter and pepperoncini.

**3.** In small bowl mix mayonnaise, vinegar, dill, and paprika. Spread over meat.

**4.** Cover and cook on Low for 8 hours. Remove from cooker, shred with forks, and return to cooker. Stir to mix juices and serve.

# Beef Roast Made Easy

*Colleen Heatwole, Burton, MI*

*Makes 8–10 servings*

*Prep. Time: 10 minutes* ⚗ *Cooking Time: 7 hours* ⚗ *Ideal slow-cooker size: 3- to 4-qt.*

3–4-lb. beef chuck roast

1 envelope dry ranch dressing mix

1 envelope dry Italian dressing mix

1 envelope dry brown gravy mix

1 cup of water

**1.** Grease or spray with vegetable cooking spray the interior of slow cooker.

**2.** Place all ingredients in the slow cooker.

**3.** Cover and cook on Low for 7 hours or until instant-read thermometer registers 140–145°F when inserted in center of roast.

*Serving suggestion:*

*Serve with potatoes, salad, and bread.*

**TIP**

With this recipe you don't need to brown the roast beforehand.

# Italian Beef Sandwiches

*Hope Comerford, Clinton Township, MI*

**Makes 6–8 servings**
Prep. Time: 5 minutes & Cooking Time: 8–10 hours & Ideal slow-cooker size: 3-qt.

3½–4½-lb. English roast

16 oz. jar pepperoncini

6–8 sub buns

butter

6–8 large slices provolone or mozzarella cheese

**1.** Place the roast into the crock and pour the jar of pepperoncini, juice and all, over the top of the roast.

**2.** Cover and cook on Low for 8–10 hours.

**3.** Remove the roast and shred it between two forks. Replace it back into the crock and stir it through the juices.

**4.** Preheat the oven to 400°F.

**5.** Place each sub bun open-faced on a foil-lined cookie sheet. Spread a bit of butter on each side. Place the cheese on top of each bun. Place them in the oven for about 8 minutes, or until the bread is slightly toasted and the cheese is melted.

**6.** Remove the sub buns from the oven and place a good portion of Italian beef on top.

## TIP
This is also good on top of nachos or a salad.

# Tuscan Roast Beef and Cheddar Melts

*MarJanita Geigley, Lancaster, PA*

**Makes 4 servings**

*Prep. Time: 30 minutes* ⚜ *Cooking Time: 2–4 hours* ⚜ *Ideal slow-cooker size: 6- to 7-qt.*

¼ cup sour cream

2 Tbsp. chives

1 Tbsp. horseradish

½ Tbsp. Dijon mustard

¾ tsp. lemon juice

⅛ tsp. salt

⅛ tsp. pepper

dash of Tabasco sauce

8 slices of Tuscan bread

2 Tbsp. oil

8 slices of cheddar cheese

12 slices of roast beef

¼ cup chopped onion

¼ cup chopped tomato

**1.** Combine first 8 ingredients in small dish to make the sauce.

**2.** Brush 1 side of the bread slices with oil.

**3.** Brush the other side of bread slices with sauce.

**4.** Place cheese, beef, and veggies on breads to make sandwiches.

**5.** Place in slow cooker on Low for 2 hours to melt.

# One-Pot Dinner

*Janie Steele, Moore, OK*

*Makes 4–6 servings*
*Prep. Time: 30 minutes* ❧ *Cooking Time: 5 hours* ❧ *Ideal slow-cooker size: 4-qt.*

1 lb. ground beef
1 cup sliced onion
salt and pepper, to taste
¼ tsp. onion powder
1 cup sliced celery
2 cups sliced carrots
2 cups sliced potatoes
10¾-oz. can condensed cream of celery soup

**1.** Brown meat and onions. Add seasonings. Drain.

**2.** Put meat and onions on bottom of slow cooker, next celery, carrots, and potatoes in layers. End with soup (do not add water).

**3.** Cover and cook on Low 5 hours.

# Meatloaf

Colleen Heatwole, Burton, MI

**Makes 6–8 servings**
Prep. Time: 15 minutes ❧ Cooking Time: 4–6 hours ❧ Ideal slow-cooker size: 6-qt.

2 lbs. ground beef

2 eggs

⅔ cup dry quick oats

½ envelope of dry onion soup mix

½–1 tsp. liquid smoke

1 tsp. ground mustard

½ cup ketchup, *divided* (reserve 2 Tbsp.)

1. Spray inside of slow cooker with cooking spray.

2. Combine all ingredients except reserved ketchup in large bowl.

3. Shape into loaf and add to slow cooker.

4. Top with remaining ketchup.

5. Cover.

6. Cook on Low 4–6 hours or until instant-read thermometer registers 160°F when inserted into center of meatloaf.

Serving suggestion:
Mashed potatoes, salad, and bread always go well with meatloaf.

## TIPS

1. An oven cooking thermometer, the kind with the probe, works well in preparing meat dishes in the slow cooker as it does in the oven.

2. This meatloaf is easier to cut if you let it cool for a bit before slicing.

3. Using a slow-cooker liner for this dish makes cleanup easier.

# Chinese Hamburger Casserole

*Linda Tyson, Brownstown, PA*

**Makes 4–6 servings**
Prep. Time: 15 minutes  &  Cooking Time: 2 hours  &  Ideal slow-cooker size: 3-qt.

1 lb. ground beef
14¾-oz. can mushroom soup
3 tbsp. milk
2 Tbsp. soy sauce
2 cups diced celery
1 pint frozen peas, thawed
¾ cup diced onion
¾ cup bread crumbs
chips or chow mein noodles

**1.** Grease crock with cooking spray.

**2.** Brown meat.

**3.** Mix mushroom soup with the milk and soy sauce.

**4.** Beginning with celery, alternate layers of celery, peas, onion, meat and soup mixture until all are used.

**5.** Top with bread crumbs. Then place chips or chow mein noodles over top.

# Hamburger Casserole

*Sharon Miller, Holmesville, OH*

**Makes 6–8 servings**

*Prep. Time: 20–30 minutes* ⚇ *Cooking Time: 6–8 hours* ⚇ *Ideal slow-cooker size: 5-qt.*

2 cups shredded potatoes

2 cups thinly sliced carrots

3 medium onions, chopped

1 cup peas, canned or frozen

2 celery stalks, diced

salt and pepper, to taste

1 lb. lean ground beef

10-oz. can low-sodium, low-fat tomato soup

10-oz. water

1. Place prepared vegetables in crock in layers; salt and pepper to taste each layer.

2. Place raw meat on top of celery.

3. Mix soup and water; pour over mixture.

4. Cover and cook on Low 6–8 hours.

Serving suggestion:

Serve with warm garlic bread.

**TIP**

Vegetables and meat can be increased by ½, if desired, but use same amount of soup and water.

# Connie's Sloppy Joes

*Carolyn Spohn, Shawnee, KS*

*Makes 8–10 servings*
Prep. Time: 15 minutes  &  Cooking Time: 4–6 hours  &  Ideal slow-cooker size: 3-qt.

2½ lbs. lean ground beef or ground turkey, or a combination of the two

¾ cup diced onion

¼ cup brown sugar

2 Tbsp. vinegar

1 tsp. prepared mustard

¼ tsp. garlic powder

⅛ tsp. black pepper

1¼ cups ketchup

¼ tsp. salt, *optional*

1. Brown meat and onion; drain well.

2. Put all ingredients in crock.

3. Cover and cook on Low 4–6 hours.

*Serving suggestion:*

*Serve on hamburger buns.*

**TIP**

If you like your sloppy joes with a bit of a kick, add in ¼ cup of your favorite spicy barbecue sauce.

# Sloppy Joes

*Hope Comerford, Clinton Township, MI*

*Makes 15–18 servings*
*Prep. Time: 25 minutes   ♣   Cooking Time: 6–7 hours   ♣   Ideal slow-cooker size: 6-qt.*

1½ lbs. lean ground beef

16 oz. mild pork sausage

½ large red onion, chopped

½ green bell pepper, chopped

8-oz. can tomato sauce

½ cup water

½ cup ketchup

¼ cup tightly packed brown sugar

2 Tbsp. apple cider vinegar

2 Tbsp. yellow mustard

1 Tbsp. Worcestershire sauce

1 Tbsp. chili powder

1 tsp. garlic powder

1 tsp. onion powder

¼ tsp. salt

¼ tsp. pepper

hamburger buns

**1.** Brown the ground beef and sausage in a pan. Drain all grease.

**2.** While the beef and sausage is cooking, mix together the remaining ingredients (except for the buns) in the crock.

**3.** Add the cooked beef and sausage to the crock and mix.

**4.** Cover and cook on Low for 6–7 hours.

**5.** Serve on hamburger buns.

# Reuben Casserole

*Janie Steele, Moore, OK*

*Makes 4–6 servings*
*Prep. Time: 30 minutes  ⚬  Cooking Time: 1½–3 hours  ⚬  Ideal slow-cooker size: 4-qt.*

1¼ cups Thousand Island dressing

1 cup sour cream

1 Tbsp. minced onion

6 slices dark rye bread, cubed

6 slices light rye bread, cubed

¾ lb. sauerkraut drained

1½ lbs. corned beef, cut into bite-size pieces

1½ lbs. shredded Swiss cheese

¼ cup margarine

**1.** Grease crock with butter or spray oil.

**2.** Mix dressing, sour cream, and onion in bowl.

**3.** Arrange bread cubes in crock (reserve ½ cup each for topping). Cover bread with sauerkraut and corned beef.

**4.** Spread dressing mixture over corned beef and sprinkle cheese over the top. Top with remaining bread. Add pats of butter on top.

**5.** Cover and cook on High for 1½ hours, or on Low for 3 hours.

# Venison Steak

*Janeen Troyer, Fairview, MI*

**Makes 5 servings**
*Prep. Time: 20 minutes* ⚜ *Cooking Time: 2 hours* ⚜ *Ideal slow-cooker size: 4-qt.*

2 venison steaks
flour
2 Tbsp. shortening
dash of pepper
14¾-oz. can of mushroom soup

**1.** Roll the steaks in the flour and then brown the steaks in the shortening on the top of the stove.

**2.** Place the steaks in a greased crock and add pepper. Cover with the mushroom soup.

**3.** Cover and cook on High for 2 hours or until done.

Serving suggestion:

Serve with baked potatoes.

# Venison Sandwiches

*Anita Troyer, Fairview, MI*

**Makes 6 servings**

*Prep. Time: 10 minutes* ⚬ *Cooking Time: 6 hours* ⚬ *Ideal slow-cooker size: 3-qt.*

3 lbs. venison boneless muscles

2 cups water

2 tsp. beef base

½ tsp. fresh minced ginger

16-oz. bottle Sweet Baby Ray's® Original Barbecue Sauce

**1.** Place all ingredients (except sauce) into a greased slow cooker and cook on High 5 hours or until well cooked. Size of muscles will determine length needed to fully cook.

**2.** Remove meat from broth and let set until cool. Remove all fat and sinew. Cut cross-grain into ½-inch lengths. Put meat into a slow cooker.

**3.** Add barbecue sauce to the meat. Add to desired sauciness. You may add a bit of the broth if desired so the meat mixture isn't too strong with tomato flavor.

**4.** Heat on Low for 1 hour and serve in buns.

**TIP**
You may add 3 Tbsp. mayonnaise right before serving to cut down on the tomato flavor.

# Spicy Pulled Pork Sandwiches

*Janie Steele, Moore, OK*

**Makes 8–10 servings**

*Prep. Time: 15–20 minutes* ⚜ *Cooking Time: 8–10 hours* ⚜ *Ideal slow-cooker size: 5-qt.*

4 lb. pork loin

14 oz. low-sodium beef broth

⅓ cup Worcestershire sauce

⅓ cup Louisiana Hot Sauce

kaiser rolls or buns of your choice

**Sauce:**

½ cup Worcestershire sauce

¼ cup hot sauce

1 cup ketchup

1 cup molasses

½ cup mustard

**1.** Cut roast in half and place in slow cooker.

**2.** Mix broth, Worcestershire sauce, and hot sauce in a bowl and add to crock.

**3.** Cover and cook 8–10 hours on Low. Remove meat, discard liquid.

**4.** Shred pork loin with two forks and return to slow cooker. Mix sauce and pour over meat and mix.

**5.** Cover and cook 30 minutes more or until heated through. Serve on buns.

# Pulled Pork

*Jenny R. Unternahrer, Wayland, IA*

**Makes 6–8 servings**
Prep. Time: 10 minutes  ❧  Cooking Time: 6–8 hours  ❧  Ideal slow-cooker size: 3-qt.

1 onion

2–3-lb. pork butt roast
(larger is okay, too)

salt and pepper, to taste

**1.** Slice onion and put ½ in the bottom of your slow cooker.

**2.** Remove meat netting (if it has that) and trim off any large pieces of fat. (There will be plenty of marbling; you don't need extra fat to dig through later.) Sprinkle with salt and pepper, add to crock, and sprinkle on other onions.

**3.** Cook on Low for 6–8 hours or until meat flakes easily with a fork. Pull out hunks of meat with tongs and place in bowl. Shred with fork (or your fingers if you are tough enough).

## TIPS

1. To store in fridge or freezer, keep the juice. Strain meat through a small sieve. Stir to coat. When ready to use, drain off the liquid; don't want to dilute your flavors.

2. Mix with barbecue sauce (homemade or bottled) and enjoy as a sandwich with creamy coleslaw as a condiment. Use as a topping on a quick pizza. Add some cumin, chili powder, and cayenne pepper and use in tostadas.

# Sweet Mustard Pulled Pork

*Jenny R. Unternahrer, Wayland, IA*

*Makes 6–10 servings*
*Prep. Time: 10 minutes* ⚘ *Cooking Time: 8–9 hours* ⚘ *Ideal slow-cooker size: 5- to 6-qt.*

1 cup yellow mustard

⅔ cup dark brown sugar

⅔ cup soy sauce (or soy-free substitute)

2 Tbsp. chili powder

½ tsp. dried onion powder

¼ cup apple cider vinegar

7-lb. pork shoulder (pork butt) roast

**1.** In small bowl, mix together all ingredients but the pork. Pour into slow cooker.

**2.** Trim pork of any large pieces of fat. Add to crock and turn to coat. Poke several times with a knife for the sauce to penetrate the roast. Cook on Low for 8–9 hours, or until meat shreds easily with a fork. Remove pork from crock and shred.

**3.** Strain sauce through a sieve and pour over the meat. The meat will soak some of the sauce back up.

Serving suggestions:

This is good served as is, or in a bun, tortilla, taco shell, or over buttered noodles with a side of cheesy veggies.

# Simple Shredded Pork Tacos

*Jennifer Freed, Rockingham, AL*

**Makes 6 servings**

*Prep. Time: 5 minutes* ❧ *Cooking Time: 8 hours* ❧ *Ideal slow-cooker size: 4-qt.*

2-lb. boneless pork roast
1 cup salsa
4-oz. can chopped green chilies
½ tsp. garlic salt
½ tsp. black pepper

**1.** Place all ingredients in slow cooker.

**2.** Cover; cook on Low 8 hours, or until meat is tender.

**3.** To serve, use 2 forks to shred pork.

Serving suggestion:
Serve with tortillas and your favorite condiments.

# Cranberry Pork Roast

Marcia S. Myer, Manheim, PA

*Makes 4–6 servings*
Prep. Time: 5 minutes  &  Cooking Time: 6–8 hours  &  Ideal slow-cooker size: 6-qt.

2½–3-lb. boneless pork loin roast
16-oz. can cranberry sauce
¼ cup sugar
½ cup cranberry juice or water
1 tsp. dry mustard
¼ tsp. ground cloves
2 Tbsp. cornstarch

**1.** Trim the fat off the pork and place into slow cooker.

**2.** Mash the cranberry sauce in a bowl. Add the sugar, cranberry juice, dry mustard, and cloves. Mix well and pour over the pork.

**3.** Cook on Low for 6–8 hours, or until the roast is tender. Transfer the roast to a plate and cover with foil to keep warm.

**4.** Skim the fat from the juices in the slow cooker. Measure 2 cups on the juice, adding water if needed to make 2 cups. Pour into a saucepan and bring to a boil over medium heat.

**5.** Mix the cornstarch in 2 Tbsp. cool water. When juice in the saucepan begins to boil, gradually add the cornstarch mixture and stir until thickened, about 4 minutes. Serve the cranberry gravy with the roast.

*Serving suggestion:*

*Mashed potatoes or noodles are good served with this recipe.*

# Pork Butt Roast

*Jessica Stoner, Plain City, OH*

**Makes 6–8 servings**
Prep. Time: 15–20 minutes ⚬ Cooking Time: 8–10 hours ⚬ Ideal slow-cooker size: 6-qt.

5-lb. pork butt
2 pkgs. dry onion soup mix
¼ cup Worcestershire sauce

1. Sear pork on all sides if you have time.

2. Place pork in crock.

3. Mix soup and Worcestershire sauce, then pour this over the roast.

4. Cover and cook on Low for 8–10 hours.

# Pork Roast and Vegetables

*Jenny R. Unternahrer, Wayland, IA*

**Makes 8–10 servings**

*Prep. Time: 15 minutes* ⚜ *Cooking Time: 6–8 hours* ⚜ *Ideal slow-cooker size: 5-qt.*

3 Tbsp. canola or olive oil

3–4 lb. boneless chuck roast, trimmed

salt and pepper, to taste

¼ cup flour

2 Tbsp. tomato paste

½ cup dry white wine

1½ cups beef or chicken broth

1 Tbsp. Worcestershire sauce

1 medium onion, thinly sliced (more or less onions as you like)

handful baby carrots

2 small ribs celery, thinly sliced

3 cloves garlic, diced

½ tsp. dried thyme

small potatoes, quartered

1. Heat oil in pan (preferable not a nonstick). Sprinkle roast with salt and pepper. Sear roast on all sides until browned, approximately 10 minutes. Place in large slow cooker.

2. Add flour and tomato paste to pan and cook for 1 minute. Add wine, broth, and Worcestershire sauce, scraping the bits off the bottom of the pan.

3. Pour over roast. Mix vegetables, garlic, and dried thyme in bowl and add to crock.

4. Cover and cook for 6–8 hours on Low. Add quartered potatoes to liquid after 4 hours. Serve in bowl so you can ladle the gravy over the top.

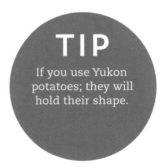

**TIP**

If you use Yukon potatoes; they will hold their shape.

# Easiest Ever BBQ Country Ribs

*Hope Comerford, Clinton Township, MI*

*Makes 4–6 servings*
*Prep. Time: 5 minutes  ⚜  Cooking Time: 8–10 hours  ⚜  Ideal slow-cooker size: 6-qt.*

4 lbs. boneless country ribs

salt and pepper, to taste

18-oz. bottle of your favorite barbecue sauce

1. Place your country ribs into your crock and sprinkle them with salt and pepper on both sides.

2. Pour half the bottle of barbecue sauce on one side of the ribs. Flip them over and poor the other half of the barbecue sauce on the other side of your ribs. Spread it around.

3. Cover and cook on Low for 8–10 hours.

# Teriyaki Pork Steak with Sugar Snap Peas

Hope Comerford, Clinton Township, MI

*Makes 4–6 servings*
Prep. Time: 10 minutes ⚜ Cooking Time: 7–9 hours ⚜ Ideal slow-cooker size: 5-qt.

2½-lb. pork shoulder blade steaks
1 Tbsp. onion powder, *divided*
1 Tbsp. garlic powder, *divided*
salt and pepper, to taste
1 cup teriyaki sauce, *divided*
½ medium onion, sliced into half rings
1½–2 cups sugar snap peas

**1.** Place the pork steaks in your crock and sprinkle them with half the onion powder, garlic powder, and a bit of salt and pepper.

**2.** Cover them with half of the teriyaki sauce.

**3.** Place your onions on top and sprinkle them with more salt, pepper, and the rest of the garlic powder and onion powder. Pour the rest of the teriyaki sauce over the top.

**4.** Cover and cook on Low for 7–9 hours.

**5.** About 40 minutes before the cook time is up, add in the sugar snap peas.

**6.** Serve the pork with some of the sugar snap peas on top and sauce from the crock drizzled over the top.

# Polish Sausage and Sauerkraut

*Hope Comerford, Clinton Township, MI*

*Makes 4–6 servings*
*Prep. Time: 25 minutes* ⚜ *Cooking Time: 6–7 hours* ⚜ *Ideal slow-cooker size: 6-qt.*

27 oz. Polish sausage, cut into 1½-inch angled pieces

4 slices of cooked bacon, chopped

2 Golden Delicious apples, peeled and cut into thin slices

2 lbs. sauerkraut, drained and rinsed well

½ of a large red onion, sliced

1 bay leaf

2 cloves garlic, minced

2 Tbsp. brown sugar

12 oz. dark beer

**1.** Place all of the ingredients into your crock, pouring the beer in last.

**2.** Cover and cook on Low for 6–7 hours.

**3.** When you are ready to serve, remove the bay leaf and discard it.

# Beer Poached Italian Sausage

*Hope Comerford, Clinton Township, MI*

**Makes 10 servings**
Prep. Time: 2 minutes    Cooking Time: 6–7 hours    Ideal slow-cooker size: 5-qt.

2 19-oz. pkgs. Italian sausage

12 oz. beer

10 hot dog buns

**1.** Place the sausage in the crock and pour the beer over the top.

**2.** Cover and cook on Low for 6–7 hours.

**3.** Serve in buns.

Serving suggestion:
Serve topped with freshly chopped onions and spicy mustard.

# Jambalaya

*Hope Comerford, Clinton Township, MI*

*Makes 4–5 servings*

*Prep. Time: 20 minutes* ♣ *Cooking Time: 8 hours* ♣ *Ideal slow-cooker size: 3-qt.*

1 lb. boneless skinless chicken, chopped into 1-inch pieces

½ lb. andouille sausage

1 large onion, chopped

1 green bell pepper, seeded and chopped

2 cups okra, chopped

1 rib celery, chopped

28-oz. can diced tomatoes

1 cup chicken broth

2 tsp. dried oregano

2 tsp. Cajun seasoning

1 tsp. salt

1 tsp. hot sauce

2 bay leaves

½ tsp. thyme

1 lb. frozen peeled and cooked shrimp, thawed

cooked rice

1. Place all of the ingredients into the crock *except* the shrimp and rice, and stir.

2. Cover and cook on Low for 8 hours.

3. Right before you are ready to serve, add the shrimp and let cook an additional 5 minutes.

4. Serve over rice.

**TIP**

Make 5-minute rice while the shrimp is cooking and everything will be ready to go all at the same time!

# Chicken Made Easy

*Colleen Heatwole, Burton, MI*

**Makes 4–6 servings**
*Prep. Time: 15 minutes* ☙ *Cooking Time: 4 hours* ☙ *Ideal slow-cooker size: 4-qt.*

6 boneless, skinless chicken thighs
1 envelope dry onion soup mix
1 cup reduced-fat sour cream
14¾-oz. can cream of chicken soup

**1.** Grease interior of slow cooker. You can use cooking spray.

**2.** Place chicken in slow cooker. If you need to make second layer, stagger pieces so they don't directly overlap each other.

**3.** In a bowl combine dry soup mix, sour cream, and chicken soup until well mixed.

**4.** Pour over chicken, making sure all pieces are covered.

**5.** Cover. Cook on Low 4 hours or until instant-read thermometer registers 165°F when inserted in center of thighs.

*Serving suggestion:*

*Serve with rice or noodles.*

# Chicken Marsala

*Hope Comerford, Clinton Township, MI*

**Makes 4–6 servings**
Prep. Time: 35 minutes ❧ Cooking Time: about 5½ hours ❧ Ideal slow-cooker size: 4-qt.

½ cup cornstarch

1 tsp. salt

1 tsp. oregano

½ tsp. pepper

½ cup or so of olive oil, *divided*

4 lbs. thinly sliced boneless skinless chicken breasts

1 large onion, halved and sliced into half-rings

12 oz. baby bella (a.k.a. portobello) mushrooms, sliced

2¼ cups Marsala wine, *divided*

1½ Tbsp. butter

½ cup milk

**1.** In a casserole dish, mix together the cornstarch, salt, pepper, and oregano.

**2.** Heat about ¼ cup of the olive oil in a large frying pan over medium heat.

**3.** Coat each side of your chicken breasts with the cornstarch mixture and place them in the frying pan until each side is slightly browned.

**4.** Place each breast into the crock.

**5.** In the same pan you just browned the chicken, add about 1½ Tbsp. olive oil and sauté the onions until they are just slightly translucent. Add in 2 cups of Marsala wine and cook on high heat for about 7 minutes, or until it thickens. Pour it over the chicken in the crock.

**6.** Cover and cook on Low for 4½ hours.

**7.** Over medium-high heat, melt the butter and remaining 1½ Tbsp. olive oil. Add in the mushrooms and cook for about 5 minutes.

**8.** Add in the remaining ¼ cup Marsala wine and whisk in the ½ cup milk. (Whisking will keep it from curdling.)

**9.** Pour the mushroom mixture over the chicken and cover and cook an additional 30 minutes.

# Slow-Cooker Chicken Fajitas

*Lisa Clark, Chesterfield, MI*

*Makes 6–8 servings*
Prep. Time: 20 minutes ⚜ Cooking Time: 3–8 hours ⚜ Ideal slow-cooker size: 3-qt.

2 lb. skinless, boneless breasts
2 peppers, sliced (red, green, or yellow)
1 large onion, sliced
1 envelope taco seasoning
10-oz. can Ro*Tel® or plain diced tomatoes
juice of 1 lime

1. Place half of the peppers and onions on bottom of crock.

2. Place chicken breasts on top of veggies.

3. Sprinkle taco seasoning on both sides of breasts.

4. Place remaining peppers and onions on top of chicken.

5. Pour tomatoes over top.

6. Squeeze lime juice over top. Cover and cook on Low 7–8 hours or High 3–4 hours.

7. If you prefer, you can shred chicken before serving or serve sliced.

Serving suggestion:

This pairs well with white rice, Spanish rice, or refried beans.

# Slow-Cooker Chicken and Salsa

*Marcia S. Myer, Manheim, PA*

*Makes 6 servings*

*Prep. Time: 10 minutes  &  Cooking Time: 4–10 hours  &  Ideal slow-cooker size: 5-qt.*

2 15-oz. cans black beans

1½ lbs. boneless chicken breasts, cut into serving-size pieces

16-oz. jar black bean salsa

16 oz. corn salsa

1 cup uncooked brown rice

2 cups water

1 cup sour cream

1 cup shredded cheddar cheese or Mexican blend cheese

1 avocado, sliced, for garnish

½ (5 oz.) pkg. corn chips, for garnish

**1.** Combine the beans, chicken, black bean salsa, corn salsa, brown rice, and 2 cups water in a slow cooker.

**2.** Cook on High for 4 hours or on Low for 8–10 hours, adding water if needed near the end of the cooking time.

**3.** To serve, place 1½ cups of the chicken mixture on individual serving plates. Top with the sour cream and cheese. Garnish with the avocado and corn chips.

# Salsa Ranch Chicken with Black Beans

*Hope Comerford, Clinton Township, MI*

*Makes 8–10 servings*

*Prep. Time: 5 minutes   ♣   Cooking Time: 5–6 hours   ♣   Ideal slow-cooker size: 5-qt.*

2–3 lbs. boneless skinless chicken breasts

1¼-oz. pkg. taco seasoning

1-oz. pkg. dry ranch dressing mix

1 cup salsa

10¾ oz. can cream of chicken soup

15½ oz. can black beans, drained and rinsed

1. Place the chicken in the bottom of your crock.

2. In a bowl, mix together the taco seasoning, ranch dressing mix, salsa, cream of chicken soup, and black beans. Pour it over the chicken.

3. Cover and cook on Low for 5–6 hours.

4. Remove the chicken and shred it between two forks. Replace the chicken back in the crock and stir.

**TIP**

To make this even more delicious, include a dollop of sour cream and some shredded cheese when serving. Black olives and sliced green onions make a nice accompaniment as well.

Serving suggestions:

This is great in tacos, on nachos, on top of a salad, on top of rice, or just on its own!

# Chicken with Spicy Sesame Sauce

Colleen Heatwole, Burton, MI

**Makes 6–8 servings**
Prep. Time: 20 minutes ⚬ Cooking Time: 4 hours ⚬ Ideal slow-cooker size: 4-qt.

6 boneless, skinless chicken breast thighs

¼ cup finely chopped onion

2 Tbsp. tahini (sesame paste)

1 tsp. red wine vinegar

2 cloves garlic, minced

1 tsp. gingerroot, finely shredded

2 Tbsp. soy sauce

1. Spray slow cooker with cooking spray.

2. Place chicken breast halves on bottom of slow cooker, trying to overlap as little as possible.

3. Soften finely chopped onion with 2 Tbsp. water in the microwave.

4. Combine softened onions, tahini, red wine vinegar, minced garlic, gingerroot, and soy sauce and pour over chicken breast halves.

5. Pour over chicken and spread sauce evenly.

6. Cook until internal temperature of chicken is 165°F on instant-read thermometer when inserted into thickest part of thighs, about 4 hours on Low.

Serving suggestions:

This sauce works fabulously to drizzle over potatoes or rice. Chicken can also be shredded for sandwiches with sauce added so it isn't dry.

## TIPS

Drain chicken and place on platter, reserving sauce. A Microplane works best for shredding the gingerroot.

# Cheesy Chicken, Bacon, Tater Tot Slow-Cooker Bake

*Kris Zimmerman, Lititz, PA*

*Makes 8–10 servings*
*Prep. Time: 15 minutes    Cooking Time: 3–4 hours    Ideal slow-cooker size: 4-qt.*

32-oz. bag Tater Tots, *divided*
3 Tbsp. real bacon bits, *divided*
1½ cups cheddar cheese
1½ cups Monterey Jack cheese
5 boneless, skinless chicken breasts
salt and pepper, to taste
¾ cup milk

1. Grease bottom of crock.

2. Layer half the potatoes on bottom of crock.

3. Sprinkle with 1½ Tbsp. of the bacon bits.

4. Combine the two cheeses, and sprinkle a third of it over the bacon potatoes.

5. Top cheese with chicken breasts.

6. Sprinkle chicken with salt and pepper.

7. Top chicken with another third of cheese.

8. Sprinkle with another 1½ Tbsp. of the bacon bits.

9. Add remainder of potatoes.

10. Top with remaining cheese.

11. Pour milk over everything.

12. Cook on High for 3–4 hours.

# Mexi-Dutch Pot Pie

*MarJanita Geigley, Lancaster, PA*

**Makes 4–5 servings**
Prep. Time: 20 minutes  &  Cooking Time: 4 hours  &  Ideal slow-cooker size: 4- to 6-qt.

2 large wheat tortilla shells

10¾-oz. can reduced-sodium cream of mushroom soup

2 cups cooked, shredded chicken

4½-oz. can chopped and drained green chilies

16-oz. bag frozen mixed vegetables

⅓ cup fresh cilantro

½ tsp. minced garlic

1 cup shredded cheese

1. Spray or grease slow cooker.

2. Lay down one shell.

3. Mix other ingredients and pour on top of shell.

4. Cover with remaining shell.

5. Cover crock and cook on Low for 4 hours.

Serving suggestion:
Serve with sour cream and guacamole.

# Cheese-Stuffed Pizza

*Phyllis Good, Lancaster, PA*

**Makes 6 servings**

Prep. Time: 30 minutes   ♣   Cooking Time: 2 hours   ♣   Standing Time: 20 minutes   ♣   Ideal slow-cooker size: 5-qt.

11- or 13-oz. pkg. refrigerated pizza dough

1½ cups shredded mozzarella, *divided*

½ cup thick pizza sauce

1 cup or less favorite pizza toppings such as chopped vegetables or cooked meat

**1.** Divide dough in half. Roll and/or stretch each piece of dough into an oval to match the size of the bottom of the crock.

**2.** Place 1 dough oval in greased slow cooker, pushing and stretching it out to the edges. Sprinkle with ½ cup mozzarella.

**3.** Place the other dough oval on top of the cheese, stretching it to the edges of the crock.

**4.** Cook, uncovered, for 1 hour on High. Dough should be puffy and getting brown at edges.

**5.** Spread pizza sauce on top. Sprinkle with remaining 1 cup cheese and any toppings you wish.

**6.** Place lid on cooker with chopstick or wooden spoon handle to vent it at one end.

**7.** Cook on High for an additional hour, until toppings are heated through.

# Slow-Cooker Pizza

*Sharon Miller, Holmesville, OK*

**Makes 8 servings**
*Prep. Time: 25 minutes  &  Cooking Time: 3 hours  &  Ideal slow-cooker size: 5-qt.*

1½ lb. Italian sausage, crumbled (or lean hamburger)

1 medium onion, chopped

8-oz. box rigatoni, cooked

1 green pepper, chopped

8-oz. can sliced mushrooms

3 oz. turkey pepperoni slices

32 oz. pizza sauce

1 cup shredded cheddar cheese

1 cup shredded mozzarella cheese

**1.** Brown together the sausage and onion.

**2.** Make 2 layers in sprayed crock. First layer is ½ of all the ingredients, in given order, beginning with the meat, and ending with ½ of the cheese.

**3.** Repeat the layers, making sure the cheese is the top layer.

**4.** Cover and cook on Low 3 hours.

## TIP

If small children will be among those eating the casserole, slice the pepperoni into halves or quarters so there are no large pieces to chew on.

# The Explorer's Casserole

*MarJanita Geigley, Lancaster, PA*

**Makes 6 servings**
*Prep. Time: 30 minutes* ⚬ *Cooking Time: 4–6 hours* ⚬ *Ideal slow-cooker size: 5-qt.*

1 lb. cooked ground beef

4 cubed potatoes

1½ cups uncooked rigatoni shells

1½ cups milk or water

1 clove garlic

2 Tbsp. olive oil

2 tsp. Italian seasoning

1 jar of Alfredo sauce

1 cup diced tomatoes

1 cup broccoli

1 cup shredded cheese

1. Mix all ingredients in slow cooker.

2. Cook on Low for 4–6 hours.

# Cousin Cindy's Spaghetti Sauce

*Carolyn Spohn, Shawnee, KS*

**Makes 8–10 servings**
Prep. Time: 15 minutes ❧ Cooking Time: 4–5 hours ❧ Ideal slow-cooker size: 4½-qt.

1–2 chopped onions
½ cup canola oil
3 Tbsp. parsley flakes
1 tsp. garlic powder
2 tsp. dried oregano
2 14¾-oz. cans tomato soup
2 4-oz. cans tomato paste
1 cup water
1 Tbsp. sugar

1. Cook onion in oil until soft.

2. Place onion and all other ingredients in slow cooker.

3. Cover and cook on Low for 4–5 hours.

Serving suggestion:
Serve over cooked spaghetti.

# Slow-Cooker Lasagna

*Marcia S. Myer, Manheim, PA*

*Makes 12–16 servings*

*Prep. Time: 25 minutes* ⚜ *Cooking Time: 4 hours* ⚜ *Ideal slow-cooker size: 4–5-qt.*

6½ cups uncooked wide egg noodles

3 Tbsp. butter

1½ lbs. ground beef

½ cup minced onion

3 cups spaghetti sauce, *divided*

¾ cups shredded mild cheese

3 cups shredded mozzarella cheese

**1.** Cook noodles, add butter, and toss to coat.

**2.** Brown beef and onion.

**3.** Spread ¼ cup sauce in the bottom of greased 4–5 qt. slow cooker.

**4.** Layer ⅓ of the noodles, ⅓ of the beef, ⅓ of the sauce, and ⅓ of the cheeses. Repeat layers 2 more times.

**5.** Cover and cook on Low for 4 hours.

# Easy Mac 'n' Cheese

*Juanita Weaver, Johnsonville, IL*

**Makes 6 servings**
*Prep. Time: 5 minutes* ⚶ *Cooking Time: 1½–2 hours* ⚶ *Ideal slow-cooker size: 4½-qt.*

2 cups of dry macaroni

4 cups milk

1 tsp. salt

a pinch or two of black pepper

4 oz. cream cheese

8 slices of American or cheddar cheese

½ tsp. dry mustard or 1 tsp. of prepared mustard

2 Tbsp. butter

4 slices of ham, cut into squares, *optional*

1. Measure all ingredients into slow cooker.

2. Turn cooker on High.

3. Cover and cook for 30 minutes, then stir lightly to evenly distribute cheeses.

4. Cook for another hour or so.

# Mac 'n' Cheese

*Judith Martin, Lebanon, PA*

**Makes 2–3 servings**
Prep. Time: 10 minutes  &  Cooking Time: 4–5 hours  &  Ideal slow-cooker size: 2-qt.

I Tbsp. butter, melted
½ tsp. salt
2 cups milk
½ tsp. pepper
I cup uncooked macaroni
¼ lb. Velveeta cheese-cubed

1. Mix together the butter, salt, milk, and pepper.

2. Place the macaroni in a greased crock with the cubed Velveeta. Pour the butter/milk mixture over the top. Stir.

3. Cover and cook on Low for 4–5 hours.

# Side Dishes & Vegetables

# Mac's Beans

*Wilma Haberkamp, Fairbank, IA* ♣ *Mabel Shirk, Mount Crawford, VA*

*Makes 6–8 servings*
*Prep. Time: 20 minutes* ♣ *Cooking Time: 4 hours* ♣ *Ideal slow-cooker size: 3- to 4-qt.*

4 slices bacon

3 15-oz. cans kidney beans, drained, or other beans of your choice

1 cup chili sauce

½ cup sliced green, or red, onions

⅓ cup brown sugar

1. In a small no-stick skillet, brown bacon until crisp. Reserve drippings. Crumble the bacon.

2. Combine all ingredients except brown sugar in slow cooker. Add bacon drippings. Sprinkle brown sugar over the top.

3. Cover and cook on Low 4 hours.

4. Serve the beans directly from your slow cooker.

# Slow-Cooked Baked Beans

*Hope Comerford, Clinton Township, MI*

**Makes 15–20 servings**

*Soaking time: 12 hours*    *Prep. Time: 10 minutes*    *Cooking Time: 12 or more hours*    *Ideal slow-cooker size: 6-qt.*

12 oz. salt pork, chopped into small strips

1 large onion, chopped

2 lbs. navy beans

¾ cup dark brown sugar

1 cup ketchup

3 Tbsp. mustard

7 cups water

**1.** Sort the beans to make sure there are no rocks or bad beans.

**2.** Soak the beans in water for 12 or more hours, with enough water to cover them plus 4 inches.

**3.** Spray your crock with nonstick spray.

**4.** Place half of the salt pork at the bottom, then half the beans, then half the onion.

**5.** In a bowl, mix together the brown sugar, ketchup, and mustard. Pour half of this over the contents of the crock.

**6.** Place the rest of the salt pork into the crock, then the remaining beans, onions, and sauce.

**7.** Pour in the 7 cups of water.

**8.** Cover and cook on Low for 12 or more hours. You will know these are done when your mixture has turned nice and brown and has thickened.

**TIP**

If you can't find salt pork, use thick-cut bacon instead.

# Calico Beans

*Judith Martin, Lebanon, PA*

*Makes 13–15 servings*

*Prep. Time: 30 minutes   &   Cooking Time: 5–12 hours   &   Ideal slow-cooker size: 6- to 7-qt.*

2-lb. can pork and beans
1-lb. can kidney beans
1 qt. green beans
¼–½ lb. fried bacon
1 medium onion, chopped
½ cup brown sugar
½ cup ketchup
½ tsp. salt
2 Tbsp. vinegar
1 Tbsp. mustard

1. Mix all ingredients in a large slow cooker.

2. Cover and cook on High for 5–6 hours, or on Low for 10–12 hours.

# Bean Casserole

*Janeen Troyer, Fairview, MI*

*Makes 6–8 servings*
*Prep. Time: 30 minutes* ⚘ *Cooking Time: 1 hour* ⚘ *Ideal slow-cooker size: 4-qt.*

16-oz. can pork and beans
16-oz. can kidney beans
1 lb. ground beef, browned
½ lb. bacon, fried
**Sauce:**
2 Tbsp. molasses
½ tsp. salt
¼ tsp. pepper
½ tsp. chili powder
¼ cup ketchup
½ cup barbecue sauce
2 Tbsp. mustard
¾ cup brown sugar

1. Mix the first four ingredients together.

2. Mix the sauce together and add to the first four ingredients.

3. Put in a greased crock and cook for 1 hour on High.

Serving suggestion:
The leftover bean casserole is wonderful served over a baked potato.

# American Beans

*Jane Geigley, Lancaster, PA*

**Makes 4–6 servings**
*Prep. Time: 30 minutes   Cooking Time: 2 hours   Ideal slow-cooker size: 3-qt.*

1 lb. ground beef, browned
16-oz. can pork and beans
16-oz. can kidney beans
1 qt. tomato juice
1 pt. corn
½ cup brown sugar
2 Tbsp. mustard
chili powder, to taste
1 tsp. salt
1 tsp. pepper

1. Pour each ingredient into slow cooker.

2. Stir, cover, and cook on High for 2 hours.

Serving suggestion:
Serve over baked potatoes or cornbread.

# Ranch Beans

*Jo Zimmerman, Lebanon, PA*

*Makes 8–10 servings*
*Prep. Time: 10 minutes* ⚜ *Cooking Time: 3–4 hours* ⚜ *Ideal slow-cooker size: 3-qt.*

16-oz. can kidney beans, rinsed and drained

16-oz. can pork and beans

15-oz. can lima beans, rinsed and drained

14-oz. can cut green beans, drained

12-oz. bottle chili sauce

⅔ cup brown sugar, packed

1 small onion, chopped

1. Combine all ingredients in slow cooker. Mix.

2. Cover and cook on High 3–4 hours.

# Rice 'n' Beans 'n' Salsa

*Heather Horst, Lebanon, PA*

**Makes 6–8 servings**
*Prep. Time: 7 minutes*   *Cooking Time: 4–10 hours*   *Ideal slow-cooker size: 3- to 5-qt.*

2 16-oz. cans black, or navy, beans, drained

14-oz. can chicken broth

1 cup uncooked long-grain white, or brown, rice

1 qt. salsa, mild, medium, or hot

1 cup water

½ tsp. garlic powder

**1.** Combine all ingredients in slow cooker. Stir well.

**2.** Cover and cook on Low 8–10 hours, or on High 4 hours.

# Creamy Chive and Onion Mashed Potatoes

*Hope Comerford, Clinton Township, MI*

**Makes 8 servings**

*Prep. Time: 15 minutes* ⚬ *Cooking Time: 4 hours* ⚬ *Ideal slow-cooker size: 3-qt.*

4 lbs. potatoes, peeled and cubed

6 cups water, or enough to cover the potatoes

2 chicken bouillon cubes

4 Tbsp. butter

¼–½ cup milk

1½–2 tsp. salt

⅛ tsp. pepper

8 oz. chive and onion cream cheese

**1.** Place the potatoes in your crock and cover with water completely. Add the bouillon cubes.

**2.** Cover and cook on High for 3–4 hours, or until they are tender with a fork.

**3.** Drain the potatoes and wash out the inside of your crock with HOT water to prevent the crock from cracking.

**4.** Return the potatoes to the crock. Add the butter, milk, salt, and pepper.

**5.** At this point you can use a potato masher or immersion blender to make your mashed potatoes as smooth or chunky as you would like them.

**6.** Next, add the cream cheese (and a bit more milk if needed until you reach your desired consistency) and mix until well-blended.

**TIP**

These are wonderful for large family gatherings and for the holidays.

# Seasoned "Baked Potatoes"

*Donna Conto, Saylorsburg, PA*

**Makes as many servings as you need**

*Prep. Time: 5 minutes* ☙ *Cooking Time: 4–10 hours* ☙ *Ideal slow-cooker size: large enough to hold the potatoes*

potatoes

olive, or vegetable, oil

Season-All® Seasoned Salt, or your choice of favorite dry seasonings

**1.** Wash and scrub potatoes. Rub each unpeeled potato with oil.

**2.** Put about 1 tsp. seasoning per potato in a mixing bowl or a plastic bag. Add potatoes one at a time and coat with seasonings.

**3.** Place potatoes in slow cooker as you finish coating them.

**4.** Cover and cook on High for 4 hours, or on Low 8–10 hours, or until potatoes are tender when jagged.

# Easy Cheese-y Potatoes

*Carol Sherwood, Batavia, NY*

**Makes 4 servings**
*Prep. Time: 20 minutes   ⚬   Cooking Time: 3–8 hours   ⚬   Ideal slow-cooker size: 4-qt.*

30-oz. pkg. frozen hash brown potatoes, partially thawed
1-lb. pkg. kielbasa, chopped
1 medium-sized onion, diced
10¾-oz. can cheddar cheese soup
1 soup can milk

**1.** Spray interior of slow cooker with nonstick cooking spray.

**2.** Place first 3 ingredients in slow cooker. Stir together.

**3.** Mix soup and milk together in a bowl, stirring until well blended. Pour into slow cooker.

**4.** Fold all ingredients together.

**5.** Cover and cook on High 3 hours, or on Low 7–8 hours.

**TIP**
This is a great dish to bring to a potluck.

# Glazed Maple Sweet Potatoes

*Jan Mast, Lancaster, PA*

**Makes 8–10 servings**

Prep. Time: 20 minutes  ❧  Cooking Time: 3–4 hours  ❧  Ideal slow-cooker size: 2-qt.

8–10 medium-sized sweet potatoes

½ tsp. salt

¾ cup brown sugar

2 Tbsp. butter

1 Tbsp. flour

¼ cup water

**1.** Cook sweet potatoes in 2–3 inches water in a large saucepan until barely soft. Drain. When cool enough to handle, peel and slice into slow cooker.

**2.** While potatoes are cooking in the saucepan, combine remaining ingredients in a microwave-safe bowl.

**3.** Microwave on High for 1½ minutes. Stir. Repeat until glaze thickens slightly.

**4.** Pour glaze over peeled, cooked sweet potatoes in slow cooker.

**5.** Cover and cook on High 3–4 hours.

**TIP**
These potatoes pair wonderfully with pork dishes.

# Sweet Cornbread

*Hope Comerford, Clinton Township, MI*

**Makes 6 servings**
Prep. Time: 10 minutes   🌿   Cooking Time: 3½–4 hours   🌿   Ideal slow-cooker size: 3-qt.

1 cup cornmeal
1 cup flour
⅔ cup sugar
2 tsp. baking powder
3 Tbsp. butter, melted
¼ cup vegetable oil
1 egg
1–2 Tbsp. honey
1 cup milk
¼ cup frozen corn, *optional*

**1.** In a bowl, mix the cornmeal, flour, sugar, and baking powder.

**2.** Next, add the melted butter, vegetable oil, egg, honey, and milk and mix it up.

**3.** Add the corn (if using) and stir again.

**4.** Grease your crock with nonstick spray and pour in the batter.

**5.** Cover and cook on Low for 3½–4 hours.

## TIP

If you know your slow cooker really well, you might notice it has a "hot spot" where it tends to cook that spot faster. When making breads or desserts, it's a good idea to cover that hot spot with aluminum foil. It will help keep your bread or dessert from burning in that spot!

# Sweet Dried Corn

*Shelia Heil, Lancaster, PA*

**Makes 14 servings**

*Prep. Time: 5 minutes* ♣ *Cooking Time: 2–2½ hours* ♣ *Ideal slow-cooker size: 4-qt.*

5 15-oz. cans whole-kernel corn, drained

1 stick (8 Tbsp.) butter, at room temperature

¾ cup brown sugar

**1.** Place corn in slow cooker. Add butter and brown sugar. Stir to combine.

**2.** Cook on High until hot, about 1½ hours. Stir. Continue cooking on Low for another 30–60 minutes, or until corn is very hot.

# Green Beans with Tomato, Bacon, and Onions

*Hope Comerford, Clinton Township, MI*

**Makes 4 servings**

*Prep. Time: 10 minutes ⚹ Cooking Time: 4 hours ⚹ Ideal slow-cooker size: 2-qt.*

2½–3 cups fresh green beans, ends snapped off, washed and halved

2 small tomatoes, chopped

1 small onion, chopped

1½ oz. fresh bacon bits

1 tsp. onion powder

1 tsp. garlic powder

½ tsp. salt

⅛ tsp. red pepper

1 chicken bouillon cube

½ cup water

**1.** In your crock, place the green beans, tomatoes, onion, bacon bits, onion powder, garlic powder, salt, and red pepper.

**2.** Give the contents of the crock a stir, tuck your bouillon cube down into the bottom, and add your water.

**3.** Cover and cook on Low for 4 hours.

# Barbecued Green Beans

*Sharon Timpe, Jackson, WI ❦ Ruth E. Martin, Loysville, PA*

*Makes 10–12 servings*
*Prep. Time: 15 minutes ❦ Cooking Time: 3–4 hours ❦ Ideal slow-cooker size: 4-qt.*

3 14½-oz. cans cut green beans (drain 2 cans completely; reserve liquid from 1 can)

1 small onion, diced

1 cup ketchup

¾ cup brown sugar

4 strips bacon, cooked crisp and crumbled

**1.** Combine green beans, diced onion, ketchup, and brown sugar in your slow cooker.

**2.** Add ⅓ cup of reserved bean liquid. Mix gently.

**3.** Cover and cook on Low 3–4 hours, until beans are tender and heated through. Stir at the end of 2 hours of cooking, if you're home.

**4.** Pour in a little reserved bean juice if the sauce thickens more than you like.

**5.** Sprinkle bacon over beans just before serving.

**TIP**

Use 1½ lbs. fresh green beans instead of canned beans. When using fresh beans, you'll need to increase the cooking time to 5–6 hours on Low depending upon how soft or crunchy you like your beans.

# Candied Carrots

*Arlene M. Kopp, Lineboro, MD*

**Makes 3–4 servings**
Prep. Time: 10 minutes  ♣  Cooking Time: 2½–3½ hours  ♣  Ideal slow-cooker size: 3-qt.

1 lb. carrots, cut into 1-inch pieces
½ tsp. salt
¼ cup water
2 Tbsp. butter
½ cup light brown sugar, firmly packed
2 Tbsp. chopped nuts

**1.** Place carrots in slow cooker. Sprinkle with salt.

**2.** Pour water in along the side of the cooker.

**3.** Cover and cook on High 2–3 hours, or until carrots are just tender. Drain.

**4.** Stir in butter. Sprinkle with sugar.

**5.** Cover and cook on High 30 minutes.

**6.** Sprinkle with nuts about 10 minutes before end of cooking time.

# Maria's Sweet-and-Sour Red Cabbage

*Carolyn Spohn, Shawnee, KS*

**Makes 6–8 servings**

*Prep. Time: 15 minutes* ⚜ *Cooking Time: 4–6 hours* ⚜ *Ideal slow-cooker size: 4-qt.*

1 small head red cabbage, sliced

1 medium onion, chopped

3 tart apples, cored and chunked

1 tsp. salt

2 Tbsp. sugar

1 cup hot water

⅓ cup apple cider vinegar

3–6 slices of cooked and crumbled bacon

2–3 Tbsp. bacon drippings

**1.** Place all ingredients in slow cooker; stir to combine.

**2.** Cover and cook on Low for 4–6 hours.

Serving suggestion:

This goes well with pork roast.

# Use Up That Zucchini!

*Colleen Heatwole, Burton, MI*

**Makes 12–15 servings**
*Prep. Time: 30 minutes* ⚬ *Cooking Time: 3–6 hours* ⚬ *Ideal slow-cooker size: 7-qt.*

12 cups diced zucchini/summer squash (any combination)

3 cups diced onion

6-oz. package seasoned stuffing mix, chicken or herb; reserve ¼ cup

12 oz. grated sharp cheddar cheese

2 14¾-oz. cans cream of chicken soup

¼ tsp. pepper, *optional*

**1.** Spray inside of large slow cooker with vegetable cooking spray. Oval shape works best.

**2.** Cook zucchini, summer squash, and onion until vegetables are softened, on Low. You will not need to add water if you cook slowly.

**3.** Combine all ingredients except reserved ¼ cup stuffing mix.

**4.** Put in slow cooker and sprinkle with reserved stuffing mix.

# Pizza-Style Zucchini

*Marcella Roberts, Denver, PA*

**Makes 6 servings**

*Prep. Time: 20 minutes* ⚬ *Cooking Time: 2½ hours* ⚬ *Ideal slow-cooker size: 4-qt.*

3 medium zucchini, mix of yellow and green, unpeeled and cut in disks

1 large tomato, diced

½ cup pizza sauce

1 cup grated mozzarella cheese

sliced black olives, *optional*

**1.** Layer zucchini in lightly greased slow cooker, alternating colors.

**2.** Mix tomato and pizza sauce together. Pour over zucchini.

**3.** Sprinkle with mozzarella and black olives (if using).

**4.** Cover and cook on High for 2 hours, until bubbly. Remove lid and cook an additional 30 minutes on High to evaporate some of the liquid.

**TIP**

Add basil, oregano, and chopped garlic if you want to really amp up the pizza flavor.

Desserts

# Blender Brownies

*Juanita Weaver, Johnsonville, IL*

**Makes 6 servings**
*Prep. Time: 5 minutes  ❖  Cooking Time: 1 hour  ❖  Ideal slow-cooker size: 4 ½-qt.*

2 cups oatmeal

¾ cup boiling water

6 oz. cream cheese (see tip below)

4 eggs

1¾ cups brown sugar

½ cup oil

2 tsp. vanilla extract

1 tsp. salt

¾ cup cocoa powder

**1.** Measure oatmeal in blender.

**2.** Pour boiling water over oatmeal.

**3.** Add remaining ingredients in order given.

**4.** Blend for 1 minute on medium speed.

**5.** Pour into large greased slow cooker.

**6.** Turn on High and cook with lid slightly cracked for 1 hour.

*Serving suggestion:*
*Sprinkle chocolate chips or nuts on top when serving if you wish.*

**TIP**
You can use cottage cheese, sour cream, or Greek yogurt in place of cream cheese.

# Chocolate Pudding Cake

*Lee Ann Hazlett, Freeport, IL   ❧   Della Yoder, Kalona, IA*

**Makes 10–12 servings**
*Prep. Time: 5–10 minutes   ❧   Cooking Time: 3–7 hours   ❧   Ideal slow-cooker size: 4-qt.*

18½-oz. pkg. chocolate cake mix

3.9-oz. pkg. instant chocolate pudding mix

2 cups (16 oz.) sour cream

4 eggs

1 cup water

¾ cup oil

1 cup semisweet chocolate chips

**1.** Combine cake mix, pudding mix, sour cream, eggs, water, and oil in electric mixer bowl. Beat on medium speed for 2 minutes. Stir in chocolate chips.

**2.** Pour into greased slow cooker. Cover and cook on Low 6–7 hours, or on High 3–4 hours, or until toothpick inserted near center comes out with moist crumbs.

Serving suggestion:

Serve with whipped cream or with ice cream if you wish.

# White Chocolate and Mixed Berry Cobbler Cake

*Hope Comerford, Clinton Township, MI*

**Makes 6 servings**

*Prep. Time: 15 minutes* ⚬ *Cooking Time: 6 hours* ⚬ *Ideal slow-cooker size: 3-qt.*

2 cups frozen mixed berries

2 tsp. vanilla extract

¼–½ cup brown sugar

18¼ oz. yellow butter cake mix (or use plain white or yellow)

1 stick butter, melted

¼–½ cup white chocolate chips

3 Tbsp. water

1. Spray the inside of your crock with nonstick cooking spray.

2. Pour the mixed berries in the bottom of the slow cooker and top with the vanilla and brown sugar.

3. In a medium-sized bowl, mix the cake mix and butter with a pastry cutter or fork until it looks crumbly.

4. Stir in the white chocolate chips.

5. Pour the cake mixture over the mixed berries in the crock.

6. Cover and cook on Low for 6 hours.

# Blueberry Swirl Cake

*Phyllis Good, Lancaster, PA*

**Makes 10–12 servings**
*Prep. Time: 15–20 minutes* ☘ *Cooking Time: 3½–4 hours* ☘ *Ideal slow-cooker size: 5-qt.*

3-oz. pkg. cream cheese, softened
18¼-oz. box white cake mix
3 eggs
3 Tbsp. water
21-oz. can blueberry pie filling

**1.** Grease and flour interior of slow cooker crock.

**2.** Beat cream cheese in a large mixing bowl until soft and creamy.

**3.** Stir in dry cake mix, eggs, and water. Blend well with cream cheese.

**4.** Pour batter into prepared crock, spreading it out evenly.

**5.** Pour blueberry pie filling over top of batter.

**6.** Swirl blueberries and batter by zigzagging a table knife through the batter.

**7.** Cover. Bake on High 3½–4 hours, or until a tester inserted into center of cake comes out clean.

**8.** Uncover, being careful to not let condensation from lid drop on finished cake.

**9.** Remove crock from cooker.

**10.** Serve cake warm or at room temperature.

# Unbelievable Carrot Cake

*Phyllis Good, Lancaster, PA*

*Makes 12–14 servings*
*Prep. Time: 15 minutes* & *Cooking Time: 3½–4 hours* & *Ideal slow-cooker size: 6- or 7-qt. oval*

2-layer spice cake mix

2 cups (½ lb.) shredded carrots

1 cup crushed pineapple with juice

3 egg whites

½ cup All-Bran cereal

Cream Cheese Frosting:

3-oz. pkg. cream cheese, softened

4 Tbsp. (half a stick) butter, softened

2 cups confectioners' sugar

vanilla milk (start with 1 Tbsp. and increase gradually if you need more)

**TIP**

No need to shred carrots if you don't have time. You can buy them already shredded! Also, if you don't have time to make your own frosting, there is no shame in purchasing pre-made frosting for this delicious cake!

1. Combine the dry cake mix, shredded carrots, crushed pineapple with juice, egg whites, and All-Bran cereal thoroughly in a big bowl.

2. Grease and flour a loaf pan.

3. Pour batter into prepared pan.

4. Cover with greased foil and place in slow cooker.

5. Cover cooker with its lid.

6. Bake on High for 3½–4 hours, or until tester inserted in center of cake comes out clean.

7. Carefully remove pan from cooker. Place on wire baking rack to cool, uncovered.

8. As the cake cools, make the frosting by mixing together the softened cream cheese and butter, confectioners' sugar, and vanilla. When well combined, stir in milk, starting with 1 Tbsp. and adding more if necessary, until the frosting becomes spreadable.

9. Frost cake when it's completely cooled.

10. Slice and serve.

# Limealicious Cake

*Hope Comerford, Clinton Township, MI*

**Makes 6 servings**

*Prep. Time: 15 minutes* ⚜ *Cooking Time: 2 hours* ⚜ *Cooling Time: 1 or more hours* ⚜ *Ideal slow-cooker size: 6-qt.*

18¼-oz. box lemon cake mix

3-oz. box lime gelatin

3 eggs

1½ cups unsweetened apple sauce

½ cup orange juice

6 Tbsp. confectioners' sugar

½ cup lime juice

**Icing:**

8 oz. cream cheese, softened

4 Tbsp. (half a stick) butter, softened

2 cups confectioners' sugar

3 Tbsp. lime juice

1. Spray your crock with nonstick spray.

2. Mix the first 5 ingredients in a bowl and pour into your crock.

3. Cover and cook on Low for 2 hours, or until a toothpick stuck in the center comes out clean.

4. Turn the slow cooker off.

5. Mix the 6 Tbsp. confectioners' sugar with the ½ cup lime juice.

6. Poke holes in the cake all over with a toothpick or straw.

7. Pour the lime juice/confectioners' sugar mixture over the top of the cake and let the cake cool.

8. Mix together all of the icing ingredients.

9. Turn your crock upside down on a serving platter or plate to remove the cake from the crock.

10. Frost your cake.

# Harvest Goodie

*MarJanita Geigley, Lancaster, PA*

**Makes 5–6 servings**
Prep. Time: 30 minutes ☙ Cooking Time: 2–4 hours ☙ Ideal slow-cooker size: 4-qt.

2 cups sliced apples
2 cups sliced peaches
¾ cup brown sugar
½ cup flour
½ cup oats
⅓ cup softened butter
¾ tsp. cinnamon
¾ tsp. nutmeg

1. Spray or grease slow cooker.

2. Place in mixed apples and peaches.

3. Mix other ingredients together and pour over top of fruit.

4. Cook on Low for 2–4 hours.

Serving suggestion:

Serve warm and with vanilla-bean ice cream or a cold glass of milk.

# Apple Peanut Crumble

*Phyllis Attig, Reynolds, IL* ❧ *Joan Becker, Dodge City, KS* ❧ *Pam Hochstedler, Kalona, IA*

**Makes 4–5 servings**
*Prep. Time: 10 minutes* ❧ *Cooking Time: 5–6 hours* ❧ *Ideal slow-cooker size: 4-qt.*

4–5 cooking apples, peeled and sliced

⅔ cup packed brown sugar

½ cup flour

½ cup quick-cooking dry oats

½ tsp. cinnamon

¼–½ tsp. nutmeg

5⅓ Tbsp. (⅓ cup) butter, softened

2 Tbsp. peanut butter

1. Place apple slices in slow cooker.

2. Combine brown sugar, flour, oats, cinnamon, and nutmeg.

3. Cut in butter and peanut butter. Sprinkle over apples.

4. Cover cooker and cook on Low 5–6 hours.

Serving suggestion:

Serve warm or cold, plain or with ice cream or whipped cream.

# Old-Timey Raisin Crisp

*Phyllis Good, Lancaster, PA*

**Makes 12 servings**

*Prep. Time: 20 minutes* ❧ *Cooking Time: 2½–3½ hours* ❧ *Standing Time: 1 hour* ❧ *Ideal slow-cooker size: 5-qt.*

1 lb. raisins

2 Tbsp. cornstarch

½ cup sugar

1 cup water

2 Tbsp. lemon juice

**Crumbs:**

1¾ cups flour

½ tsp. baking soda

1 cup brown sugar

¼ tsp. salt

1½ cups dry oats, quick or rolled

12 Tbsp. (1½ sticks) butter

## TIP

Don't skip the lemon juice. It makes sure the crisp isn't super-sweet. Add a little more if you'd like to really taste it.

**1.** Grease interior of slow-cooker crock.

**2.** In a saucepan, combine raisins, cornstarch, sugar, and water. Cook until slightly thickened, stirring continually.

**3.** Remove from heat, stir in lemon juice, and let cool for an hour.

**4.** Prepare crumbs by combining flour, baking soda, brown sugar, salt, and dry oats in a good-sized bowl until well mixed.

**5.** Cut butter into chunks. Work into dry ingredients with your fingers, 2 knives, or a pastry cutter until fine crumbs form.

**6.** Divide crumbs in half. Spread half into bottom of slow-cooker crock. Press down to form crust.

**7.** Spoon raisin mixture over crumb crust.

**8.** Cover with remaining half of crumbs.

**9.** Cover. Bake on High 2–3 hours, or until firm in middle and bubbly around the edges.

**10.** Remove lid carefully and quickly so drops of water from inside the lid don't drip on the crisp.

**11.** Continue baking 30 more minutes to allow the crisp to dry on top.

**12.** Remove crock from cooker and place on baking rack.

**13.** Cut into squares, or spoon out of crock, to serve when warm or at room temperature.

# Banana Pecan Bars

*Phyllis Good, Lancaster, PA*

*Makes 28 servings*
*Prep. Time: 20–30 minutes   ⚘   Cooking Time: 2–2½ hours   ⚘   Ideal slow-cooker size: 6-qt. oval*

½ cup chopped pecans

2 cups flour

2 tsp. baking powder

⅛ tsp. cinnamon

2–3 very ripe bananas, enough to make 1 cup when smooshed

¼ cup shortening, at room temperature

1 cup sugar

2 eggs

1 tsp. vanilla extract

**Glaze:**

½ lb. (rounded 1 cup) confectioners' sugar

1 tsp. rum extract

a shy 2 Tbsp. water or orange juice

**1.** Grease interior of slow-cooker crock.

**2.** Combine pecans, flour, baking powder, and cinnamon.

**3.** Using a fork, smoosh ripe bananas in a good-sized bowl, enough to equal 1 cup.

**4.** Cream bananas, shortening, and sugar together.

**5.** Stir in eggs and vanilla, mixing thoroughly.

**6.** Add dry ingredients to wet, stirring until just combined.

**7.** Spread batter into greased crock.

**8.** Cover. Bake on High 2–2½ hours, or until tester inserted in center comes out clean.

**9.** Uncover. Remove crock from cooker and place on wire baking rack to cool.

**10.** While bars are cooling, make glaze. Combine confectioners' sugar and rum extract. Stir in just enough water or juice to make glaze pourable.

**11.** Drizzle glaze over bars. Then cut into 24 squares and 4 triangles in the corners.

# Easy Chocolate Clusters

*Marcella Stalter, Flanagan, IL*

**Makes 3½ dozen clusters**

*Prep. Time: 5 minutes* ⚜ *Cooking Time: 2 hours* ⚜ *Ideal slow-cooker size: 4-qt.*

2 lbs. white coating chocolate, broken into small pieces

2 cups semisweet chocolate chips

4-oz. pkg. sweet German chocolate

24-oz. jar roasted peanuts

**1.** Combine coating chocolate, chocolate chips, and German chocolate. Cover and cook on High 1 hour. Reduce heat to Low and cook 1 hour longer, or until chocolate is melted, stirring every 15 minutes.

**2.** Stir in peanuts. Mix well.

**3.** Drop by teaspoonfuls onto waxed paper. Let stand until set. Store at room temperature.

**TIP**
Try these with cashews in place of the peanuts.

# Rice Pudding

*Hope Comerford, Clinton Township, MI*

**Makes 6 servings**
Prep. Time: 5 minutes   ❧   Cooking Time: 3 hours   ❧   Standing Time: 30 minutes   ❧   Ideal slow-cooker size: 3-qt.

3 eggs, beaten
3⅓ cups milk
¼ tsp. nutmeg
¾ cup sugar
2 tsp. vanilla extract
1 cup Arborio rice
4 Tbsp. butter

**1.** Spray the crock with nonstick spray

**2.** Place the beaten eggs, milk, nutmeg, sugar, and vanilla in the crock. Mix gently.

**3.** Pour the rice in as evenly as possible and add in the butter.

**4.** Cover and cook on Low for about 3 hours. During the last hour, stir every 20 minutes or so.

**5.** Turn the slow cooker off and let the rice pudding sit in there with the lid on for about another half hour or so.

Serving suggestion:
Serve with a sprinkle of cinnamon and a dollop of whipped cream.

# Easy Rice Pudding

*Michele Ruvola, Vestal, NY*

**Makes 6 servings**
*Prep. Time: 5 minutes* ⚬ *Cooking Time: 4 hours* ⚬ *Ideal slow-cooker size: 5-qt.*

2 quarts whole milk
1 cup Arborio rice, uncooked
1 cup sugar
3 Tbsp. butter
1 tsp. vanilla extract
½ tsp. ground cinnamon
dash salt

1. Combine ingredients in slow cooker. Stir.

2. Cover and cook on Low for 4 hours, until creamy and thickened. Serve warm or chilled.

## Variations:

Add raisins, nuts, or cranberries for different variations of pudding. Add ½ tsp. ground cardamom for another variation. For an adult version, add rum-soaked raisins to pudding and cook for 15 minutes more to heat through. You can use vanilla soy milk in place of cow's milk, although the pudding will be less creamy.

# Real Tapioca Pudding

*Ruthie Schiefer, Vassar, MI*

**Makes 4–6 servings**
Prep. Time: 10 minutes ♣ Cooking Time: 2½ hours ♣ Ideal slow-cooker size: 3-qt.

½ cup small pearl tapioca
4 cups 2% milk, room temperature
¾ cup sugar
½ tsp. vanilla extract
pinch salt
2 large eggs

1. Place tapioca, milk, sugar, vanilla, and salt in slow cooker. Stir.

2. Cover and cook on Low for 2 hours.

3. In mixing bowl, thoroughly whisk eggs.

4. Continue whisking and add a large spoonful of hot tapioca mixture. Once combined, add another hot spoonful and whisk well. This prevents eggs from curdling in the next step.

5. Thoroughly fold egg mixture into remaining tapioca mixture in slow cooker.

6. Cover. Turn to High and let cook 30 additional minutes, stirring every 10 minutes, or until tapioca pearls are plump and translucent and pudding is thick.

7. Serve warm or chilled.

# Pumpkin Pudding

*Anita Troyer, Fairview, MI*

**Makes 4 servings**
Prep. Time: 15 minutes ❧ Cooking Time: 3–4½ hours ❧ Ideal slow-cooker size: 2-qt.

15-oz. can pumpkin
¾ cup white sugar
2 eggs, beaten
2 tsp. vanilla extract
12-oz. can evaporated milk
½ cup Bisquick®
2 tsp. pumpkin pie spice

**1.** Put all ingredients into greased crock. Mix well.

**2.** Cover and cook on Low for 4½ hours or on High for 3 hours.

Serving suggestion:

Serve warm with ice cream or whipped topping.

# Marshmallow Applesauce Dessert

*Marla Folkerts, Holland, OH*

**Makes 6–8 servings**

Prep. Time: 5 minutes ❧ Cooking Time: 1½–4 hours ❧ Ideal slow-cooker size: 4-qt.

4 cups applesauce
¼ tsp. allspice
½ tsp. cinnamon
2 cups mini-marshmallows

**1.** Spray slow cooker with nonfat cooking spray.

**2.** In the cooker, mix applesauce, allspice, and cinnamon together.

**3.** Sprinkle marshmallows on top.

**4.** Cook on Low 3–4 hours, or on High 1½–2 hours.

Serving suggestion:

This is delicious over ice cream and cake. It's even great as a fondue for fruit.

# Caramel-Dipped Apples

*Jane Geigley, Lancaster, PA*

**Makes 8–10 apples**

Prep. Time: 30 minutes　⚘　Cooking Time: 2 hours　⚘　Cooling Time: 10–15 minutes　⚘　Ideal slow-cooker size: 2-qt.

1 cup butter

2 cups brown sugar

1 cup corn syrup

14-oz. can sweetened condensed milk

2 tsp. vanilla extract

½ tsp. cinnamon

8–10 apples on wooden sticks

**1.** Combine all ingredients in slow cooker except for apples.

**2.** Cook on Low for 2 hours.

**3.** Dip apples into caramel blend and set on buttered waxed paper to cool.

## TIP

Dip apples into boiling water to remove wax so caramel sticks better. For a fun twist, sprinkle on chocolate chips, pecans, coconut, or other toppings after apples have been dipped in caramel mixture.

# Bold Butterscotch Sauce

*Margaret W. High, Lancaster, PA*

**Makes 16 servings**
*Prep. Time: 10 minutes* ⚜ *Cooking Time: 2–3 hours* ⚜ *Ideal slow-cooker size: 3-qt.*

8 Tbsp. (1 stick) salted butter

1 cup dark brown sugar, packed

1 cup heavy cream

½ tsp. salt, or more to taste

2 tsp. vanilla extract, or more to taste

**1.** Cut butter in slices. Add to heatproof bowl that will fit in your slow cooker.

**2.** Add sugar, cream, and salt.

**3.** Add water to crock and place bowl with butter mixture in crock so that water comes halfway up its sides.

**4.** Cover and cook on High for 2–3 hours, until sauce is steaming hot.

**5.** Wearing oven mitts to protect your knuckles, remove hot bowl from cooker.

**6.** Add vanilla. Stir. Taste. Add more vanilla and/ or salt to achieve a bold butterscotch flavor.

**TIP**
Store butterscotch in lidded jar in fridge for several weeks. Warm and stir before serving.

# Hot Fudge Sauce

*Marlene Fonken, Upland, CA*

*Prep. Time: 10 minutes* ⚘ *Cooking Time: 2½ hours* ⚘ *Ideal slow-cooker size: 1- to 3-qt.*

1 cup sugar
⅓ cup baking cocoa
2 Tbsp. flour
¼ tsp. salt
1 cup boiling water
1 Tbsp. butter, melted
1 tsp. vanilla extract

**1.** Grease interior of slow-cooker crock.

**2.** Place all ingredients in slow cooker and stir together.

**3.** Cover and cook on High 30 minutes.

**4.** Stir with a whisk to eliminate any lumps and to keep from sticking on the bottom.

**5.** Cover. Cook on Low 30 minutes.

**6.** Stir again with a whisk to remove lumps and prevent sticking.

**7.** Cover. Cook on Low 1½ hours.

**8.** Stir and serve warm over ice cream, pound cake, apple or strawberry slices, or banana chunks.

# Metric Equivalent Measurements

If you're accustomed to using metric measurements, I don't want you to be inconvenienced by the imperial measurements I use in this book.

Use this handy chart, too, to figure out the size of the slow cooker you'll need for each recipe.

## Weight (Dry Ingredients)

| | | |
|---|---|---|
| 1 oz | | 30 g |
| 4 oz | ¼ lb | 120 g |
| 8 oz | ½ lb | 240 g |
| 12 oz | ¾ lb | 360 g |
| 16 oz | 1 lb | 480 g |
| 32 oz | 2 lb | 960 g |

## Slow-Cooker Sizes

| | |
|---|---|
| 1-quart | 0.96 l |
| 2-quart | 1.92 l |
| 3-quart | 2.88 l |
| 4-quart | 3.84 l |
| 5-quart | 4.80 l |
| 6-quart | 5.76 l |
| 7-quart | 6.72 l |
| 8-quart | 7.68 l |

## Volume (Liquid Ingredients)

| | | |
|---|---|---|
| ½ tsp | | 2 ml |
| 1 tsp | | 5 ml |
| 1 Tbsp | ½ fl oz | 15 ml |
| 2 Tbsp | 1 fl oz | 30 ml |
| ¼ cup | 2 fl oz | 60 ml |
| ⅓ cup | 3 fl oz | 80 ml |
| ½ cup | 4 fl oz | 120 ml |
| ⅔ cup | 5 fl oz | 160 ml |
| ¾ cup | 6 fl oz | 180 ml |
| 1 cup | 8 fl oz | 240 ml |
| 1 pt | 16 fl oz | 480 ml |
| 1 qt | 32 fl oz | 960 ml |

## Length

| | |
|---|---|
| ¼ in | 6 mm |
| ½ in | 13 mm |
| ¾ in | 19 mm |
| 1 in | 25 mm |
| 6 in | 15 cm |
| 12 in | 30 cm |

# Recipe and Ingredient Index

# About the Author

Hope Comerford is a mom, wife, elementary music teacher, blogger, recipe developer, public speaker, FitAddict Training fit leader, Young Living Essential Oils essential oil enthusiast/educator, and published author. In 2013, she was diagnosed with a severe gluten intolerance and since then has spent many hours creating easy, practical, and delicious gluten-free recipes that can be enjoyed by both those who are affected by gluten and those who are not.

Growing up, Hope spent many hours in the kitchen with her Meme (grandmother) and her love for cooking grew from there. While working on her master's degree when her daughter was young, Hope turned to her slow cookers for some salvation and sanity. It was from there she began truly experimenting with recipes and quickly learned she had the ability to get a little more creative in the kitchen and develop her own recipes.

In 2010, Hope started her blog, *A Busy Mom's Slow Cooker Adventures*, to simply share the recipes she was making with her family and friends. She never imagined people all over the world would begin visiting her page and sharing her recipes with others as well. In 2013, Hope self-published her first cookbook, *Slow Cooker Recipes 10 Ingredients or Less and Gluten-Free*, and then later wrote *The Gluten-Free Slow Cooker*.

Hope became the new brand ambassador and author of Fix-It and Forget-It in mid-2016. She is excited to bring her creativeness to the Fix-It and Forget-It brand. Through Fix-It and Forget-It, she has written *Fix-It and Forget-It Lazy & Slow, Fix-It and Forget-It Healthy Slow Cooker Cookbook*, and *Fix-It and Forget-It Favorite Recipes for Mom*.

Hope lives in the city of Clinton Township, Michigan, near Metro Detroit. She's been a native of Michigan her whole life. She has been happily married to her husband and best friend, Justin, since 2008. Together they have two children, Ella and Gavin, who are her motivation, inspiration, and heart. In her spare time, Hope enjoys traveling, singing, cooking, reading books, spending time with friends and family, and relaxing.

# FIX-IT and FORGET-IT®